Cambridge Elements

Elements in Current Archaeological Tools and Techniques
edited by
Hans Barnard
Cotsen Institute of Archaeology
Willeke Wendrich
Polytechnic University of Turin

ARCHAEOLOGICAL WOOD AND WOODWORKING

Caroline Arbuckle MacLeod
St Thomas More College, University of Saskatchewan

Shaftesbury Road, Cambridge CB2 8EA, United Kingdom

One Liberty Plaza, 20th Floor, New York, NY 10006, USA

477 Williamstown Road, Port Melbourne, VIC 3207, Australia

314–321, 3rd Floor, Plot 3, Splendor Forum, Jasola District Centre, New Delhi – 110025, India

103 Penang Road, #05–06/07, Visioncrest Commercial, Singapore 238467

Cambridge University Press is part of Cambridge University Press & Assessment, a department of the University of Cambridge.

We share the University's mission to contribute to society through the pursuit of education, learning and research at the highest international levels of excellence.

www.cambridge.org
Information on this title: www.cambridge.org/9781009598040

DOI: 10.1017/9781009053815

© Caroline Arbuckle MacLeod 2025

This publication is in copyright. Subject to statutory exception and to the provisions of relevant collective licensing agreements, no reproduction of any part may take place without the written permission of Cambridge University Press & Assessment.

When citing this work, please include a reference to the DOI 10.1017/9781009053815

First published 2025

A catalogue record for this publication is available from the British Library

ISBN 978-1-009-59804-0 Hardback
ISBN 978-1-009-05458-4 Paperback
ISSN 2632-7031 (online)
ISSN 2632-7023 (print)

Additional resources for this publication at www.cambridge.org/macleod

Cambridge University Press & Assessment has no responsibility for the persistence or accuracy of URLs for external or third-party internet websites referred to in this publication and does not guarantee that any content on such websites is, or will remain, accurate or appropriate.

Archaeological Wood and Woodworking

Elements in Current Archaeological Tools and Techniques

DOI: 10.1017/9781009053815
First published online: March 2025

Caroline Arbuckle MacLeod
St Thomas More College, University of Saskatchewan

Author for correspondence: Caroline Arbuckle MacLeod,
carbuckle@stmcollege.ca

Abstract: Wood is, and always has been, one of the most common and versatile materials for creating structures and art. It is therefore also a ubiquitous element of the archaeological record. This discussion of the study of archaeological wood introduces a number of approaches to the analysis of these organic remains, including a brief overview of wood science, factors that impact the survival of wood materials, wood anatomy, and dendrochronology. These sections are intended to help archaeologists and other interested non-specialists prepare to encounter archaeological woods, and to understand the potential scientific data that these remains could contribute to our understanding of the human past. This is followed by additional approaches from the social sciences. The study of woodworking techniques and toolmarks, combined with ethnoarchaeology and experimental archaeology, can push wood analyses further. A combination of these approaches can help to create a more holistic view of humankind's relationship to wood.

This Element also has a video abstract: www.cambridge.org/EATT_Macleod

Keywords: archaeology, wood, dendrochronology, Egyptian coffins, archaeobotany

© Caroline Arbuckle MacLeod 2025

ISBNs: 9781009598040 (HB), 9781009054584 (PB), 9781009053815 (OC)
ISSNs: 2632-7031 (online), 2632-7023 (print)

Contents

1 Introduction: The Study of Ancient Wood — 1

2 A Brief Introduction to the Science of Wood — 5

3 The Sources, Survival, and Sample Recovery of Archaeological Wood — 12

4 The Approach to Taxonomic Assessment of Archaeological Wood and Charcoal — 24

5 Dendrochronology and Tree-Ring Research in Archaeology — 39

6 Assessing Ancient Woodworking — 48

7 Case Studies: Analyzing Wooden Coffins in Museums and in the Field — 60

8 Final Thoughts — 74

References — 76

1 Introduction: The Study of Ancient Wood

Trees are a vital resource for humankind. They provide shade, food, and air. They live, and grow, and through their growth, they record the history of the environment. They bear witness to changes in the earth, and over millennia, changes to humans and our interactions with our world. Throughout history, in almost every global region, humans have cut down these living trees in order to acquire wood for construction and craft. From virtually our earliest moments on earth, humans have been logging and using timber products for fuel and to create houses, tombs, coffins, monumental poles, figurines, baskets, clothing, and more. We have come to understand that certain woods are more desirable for certain objects, and have traded timbers with each other across vast distances. As a versatile, and generally easily worked material, wood has been integrated into virtually all aspects of our lives. It is used in both mundane and religious spheres, in times of peace and war, by our kings and the humblest members of our communities. Within the archaeological record, the remains of wooden objects therefore have the potential to provide insight into many elements of the human experience and the history of our relationship with the environment.

Unfortunately, as a generally soft, organic material, wooden objects do not often survive intact in archaeological contexts. Remains are instead usually fragmentary. Too frequently their stories are reduced to traces that only hint at what these splinters of wood or bits of charcoal may have once been, and to whom they may have once belonged. These pieces are therefore less likely to be selected for display in fine museums among the marble statues, golden masks, or even perfectly preserved ceramics that might otherwise characterize ancient cultures (Tegel et al. 2022, 1). Even more debilitating for archaeology, these less than perfect remnants of the past were often disregarded by early explorers or less systematic practitioners of our profession. They were instead usually abandoned with broken wares in refuse heaps, left to rapidly decay, exposed to air after being preserved for centuries by protective layers of sand, stone, or mud. Luckily, modern archaeologists are now more aware of the need to complete holistic analyses, combining the traces of human activities in order to begin to piece together an image of life in the past. As one of the most common organic components of the archaeological record, it is therefore vital that archaeologists understand the incredible potential insights that wooden remains can provide, even if only as fragments.

As with so many aspects of the discipline of archaeology, the study of historical and archaeological woods, or *dendroarchaeology*, can be both humanistic and scientific, in the broadest sense of these terms (Tegel et al. 2022, 2).

The strongest studies of wooden material demonstrate the importance of considering both elements, and are truly interdisciplinary (Newsom 2022, 2). From a scientific perspective, the wooden fragments make up part of the macrobotanical remains studied within *paleoethnobotany*, or *archaeobotany*. These are related terms that refer to the study of plant remains in order to understand both the ancient environment and the interactions between people and plants in the past (Pearsall 2015, 27; Stuart 2020, 8312–13). To give just a few examples, these scientific approaches involve methods for identifying wood species, quantifying samples, and different means for dating wooden specimens. This includes, of course, the large subdisciplines of dating through tree-rings, *dendrochronology*, and the study of charcoal remains, *anthracology*. As an aspect of the material record, wooden objects can also reveal information about woodworking craft and technology, serve as examples of artistic developments, reveal information about transport, exchange, architecture, and so much more.

The study of both modern and archaeological wood fragments has received considerable attention in the last few years, with more emphasis on the scientific study of the material. The following provide some examples of the types of work available, but an exhaustive literary review is beyond the scope of the present discussion (see, however, Newsom 2022, 24–32). From the scientific side, Pearsall's *Paleoethnobotany: A Handbook of Procedures* (2015), serves as an introduction to the subject. This includes the analysis of archaeological wood within a section on macroremains. Works on wood anatomy in general or for specific global regions are too numerous to discuss here, and will be examined in Section 4; however, the publications of the International Association of Wood Anatomists (1989; 2004) are worth briefly noting as they are fundamental for this discipline and consider variations in archaeological materials. A number of other edited volumes with specific sections on wood analysis and conservation have provided additional insights on specific topics (Rowell and Barbour 1989; Broda and Hill 2022; Marston et al. 2014). These works are more concerned with the approach to wood analysis or paleoethnobotany in general, rather than discussions of regional projects or the types of social inferences these studies could afford.

A number of excellent studies of wood and charcoal remains have been published as individual articles related to specific sites (Mobley and Lewis 2009; Marston 2009; Cartwright 2016, 2020; Veal 2017; Martín Seijo et al. 2021). There are, however, very few larger-scale publications dedicated to the social significance of wood use in the ancient world. I should highlight, however, the work of John Morton Coles. He contributed a number of articles and book chapters to discussions of prehistoric woodworking, particularly related to his work on wetsites at Somerset in his multi-volume series, *Somerset Levels*

Papers (1975–1989). An exceptional example of a monograph that examines ancient wood and wood use is Russell Meiggs' *Trees and Timber in the Ancient Mediterranean World* (1982). This work includes some discussion of wood analysis, but is particularly interested in textual sources for wood use. Works such as Hilary Stewart's (1995) *Cedar: Tree of Life to the Northwest Coast Indians*, and Mechtild Mertz's (2016) *Wood and Traditional Woodworking in Japan*, serve as examples of monographs that focus on the social importance of wood use in specific regions, but do not include significant references to wood science.

Some more accessible introductions to examining wood and woodworking include two illustrated books by Bruce Hoadley (2000, 1990). These include references to historical wood, but are intended as an introduction to wood science for modern wood anatomists and enthusiasts. The recent monograph by Ann Newsom (2022), *Wood in Archaeology*, provides an exceptional, more accessible introduction to archaeological wood analysis. Her discussion is unique in that she also includes sections on woodworking and examples of the types of social inferences that can be drawn based on the results of wood analysis. While the present work follows in Newsom's footsteps in many ways, her work is more in-depth and despite being slightly more holistic, remains focused on the scientific elements of archaeological wood.

The purpose of this Element is to introduce archaeologists and scholars or enthusiasts of related subjects to the multifaceted world of archaeological wood analysis. This includes the scientific study of remains for identification, dating, and interpreting historical ecology. An attempt has been made to balance this alongside anthropological approaches such as the study of ancient woodworking techniques, and what this can tell us about the related communities of woodworkers and wooden object consumers. This Element is designed to help excavators or museum professionals understand when specialists should be approached, and what the usual protocols and requirements are for in-depth investigations of wooden remains. It is intended as an accessible introduction to the basics in simplified language, but should not be considered an exhaustive survey of this complicated topic. While examples have been selected from different global regions, the case studies in Section 7 are drawn from the author's experience of working with the remains of ancient Egyptian wooden coffins. The international history of archaeological wood is too vast to do justice to the topic in this short overview, and so interested readers are encouraged to investigate the aforementioned list of publications or the selection of further readings that has been provided for each section of this work.

This Element is designed to provide an overview of wood science, before moving to additional humanistic insights. The more scientific sections, 2–5, are designed to follow the logical progression from the natural creation of trees and wood, through recovery, identification, and interpretation (as followed for instance in Pearsall 2015, 35). Following this introduction, in Section 2, I therefore define what is meant by "wood" as a technical term, and provide a simplified overview to tree growth, the development of woody plants, and the basics of wood chemistry. This fundamental background knowledge describes wood in its natural form as part of a tree, which has a significant impact on why and how it comes to be used and deposited by humans as a construction material.

Section 3 focuses on the recovery of archaeological wooden material. Here I provide an overview of the environmental and anthropological factors that impact the survival of wood in the archaeological record. This includes different types of rot and decay, as well as the means by which wood might survive these degenerative processes. Both the threats to wood and the elements that could enable its survival are of course contextually dependent. Archaeologists should be aware of what they could expect to find in their locales, and what might impact the viability of wood samples. This chapter concludes with a discussion of how to collect and store wooden finds, to ensure that they survive for further analysis.

The various approaches to wood species identification will be explored in Section 4. This will focus on identification based on wood anatomy through microscopy, as the most popular approach to wood identification in field archaeology. The reader will learn about some basic identification techniques, including how to differentiate between hardwood and softwood species, and some examples of what wood anatomists are looking for in order to arrive at species-level identifications. While this is not meant to provide a step-by-step guide to identification, it should help demonstrate what types of wood samples archaeologists should collect, and what might impact a specialist wood anatomist's chances of success.

Section 5 will focus on the topic of dendrochronology – examining the archaeological information provided by tree-rings. This will consist of a brief history of the method, and how tree-rings can be used in select instances to date objects and contexts, and to explore questions about the climate and broader environment. Basic considerations are discussed in order to help archaeologists reflect on whether this dating method might be an option for their archaeological wooden materials. A selection of common and relevant challenges that tend to arise repeatedly in the work of non-specialists, such as the "old wood problem," will be explored.

In the final two sections, I move on to the more humanistic approaches and case studies. In Section 6, I provide a brief overview of the different methods used for accessing information related to ancient woodworking practices. Some elements of wood analysis that are often overlooked by non-specialists such as seasoning and initial conversion methods are reviewed, before moving on to an overview of some of the most common woodworking tools that are found throughout history. I will explain how some of the tool marks left by these tools can be assessed, and provide a brief overview of the types of insights these examinations can provide. Some of the most common joining techniques are also described, largely to provide useful terminology to scholars working on particularly well-preserved wooden objects. Approaches from experimental archaeology and ethnoarchaeology can also help archaeologists gain access to the dynamic elements preserved within static ancient wood fragments. Some of the benefits and drawbacks to these approaches will be discussed, drawing on some of the author's own experiences.

In Section 7, I provide two case studies, focusing on my own research that involves wood analysis in two different contexts – working on ancient Egyptian wooden coffins in the Denver Museum of Nature and Science, and in the field in Saqqara, Egypt. This section, drawing on a number of the topics explored in previous chapters, helps to demonstrate that material specialists must often adapt their approach to different constraints. As with the analysis of many archaeological materials, there are often limits on access to objects or instrumentation that force plans to change, and can limit potential results. In this section, I therefore endeavour to demonstrate that the practical realities of working with wooden remains are often variable, and while frustrations do occur, the result is usually well worth the effort.

I end this Element with some brief final thoughts in Section 8. I remind the reader to keep in mind all the potential that archaeological wooden remains represent. Too often only part of the story of these fragments is told. Through more holistic analyses, however, we can uncover much more about human history, trees, and the ancient and not so ancient world.

2 A Brief Introduction to the Science of Wood

One of the most important things to remember when considering wood remains is that wood comes from trees, and trees are living organisms. Trees therefore grow, they are impacted by their environment, can be wounded, heal, and die. How trees produce wood, and how the physical, anatomical, and chemical characteristics of wood can change and develop has an impact on the preservation of archaeological wood and its subsequent analysis. In this section, I therefore introduce the science of wood. I discuss what wood is, technically speaking, and explain the basic elements of tree growth, wood production, and wood chemistry. It is important to understand these fundamental aspects of tree growth before moving on to the subsequent sections of this Element. For more thorough discussions of each topic, see the Further Reading selection in Section 2.6.

2.1 Tree Growth

Just as with most organisms, trees go through different phases of growth. These are generally referred to as juvenile, mature, and senescent stages. Each stage is associated with different characteristics (Newsom 2022, 76). During the juvenile or primary stage, when trees are starting to grow, roots and shoots develop through cell production in a part of the tree called the *apical meristem*. A meristem is a region of embryonic plant tissues that are actively going through cell division. The cell production in the shoot apical meristem is responsible for the vertical growth of the main stem of the tree. The apical meristem remains at the top of the tree, and just below it, it produces a series of additional meristems, one of which is called the *procambium*. Within the procambium, cells generally develop to become part of one of two systems: inner cells become what is referred to as the *primary xylem*, and the outer cells become the *primary phloem* (Raven et al. 2013, 585). In the last stage of this primary development the remaining elements of the procambial tissue will form a layer between the primary xylem and phloem. This layer starts to produce new cells in the secondary, or mature, growth period. This layer is now the *vascular cambium*. The vascular cambium produces the *secondary xylem* and *secondary phloem*, which become what we know of as wood and bark, respectively (Shmulsky and Jones 2011, 12). The simplified flowchart in Figure 1 provides an overview of the systems involved in this process (see Raven et al. 2013, 635, fig. 26–30, for a more complete version connected to other systems). The apical meristem continues to produce new cells during periods of growth, moving upwards. It allows the vascular cambium to remain at more or less the same height, where it continues with the lateral (outwards) growth of the tree through the production of the secondary xylem and phloem, wood and bark (Newsom 2022, 94). This is why, if you carve your initials on the trunk of a tree, they will

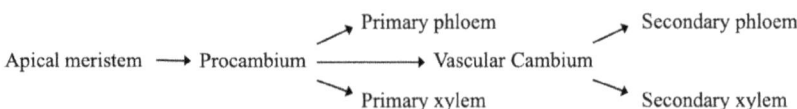

Figure 1 A simplified summary of tree growth related to the production of the secondary xylem

remain at approximately the same height, while the tree continues to grow vertically.

It should be noted that there are a number of plants that we often refer to as trees that do not go through the secondary production processes, and therefore technically do not produce wood, as they have no secondary xylem (Raven et al. 2013, 584). This includes monocots such as palm trees, for instance. A "tree" is defined as a woody plant that grows to at least 4–6 m in height. Those that are smaller are classified as shrubs or bushes (Shmulsky and Jones 2011, 3).

2.2 The Production of the Secondary Xylem: Wood

As noted previously, technically speaking, "wood" refers to the tissue system called the *secondary xylem*. We just learned that this is produced during the mature phase of tree growth. To reiterate, the cells of the secondary xylem are produced towards the interior of the tree by the meristematic tissue referred to as the vascular cambium (see Figure 2). Towards the outside of the tree, the vascular cambium is producing the cells of the secondary phloem, the inner bark of the tree (Newsom 2022, 10). This means that trees do not grow from the centre outward, as is often presumed. Instead, rings of wood are being added just to the interior of the inner bark. The vascular cambium is therefore

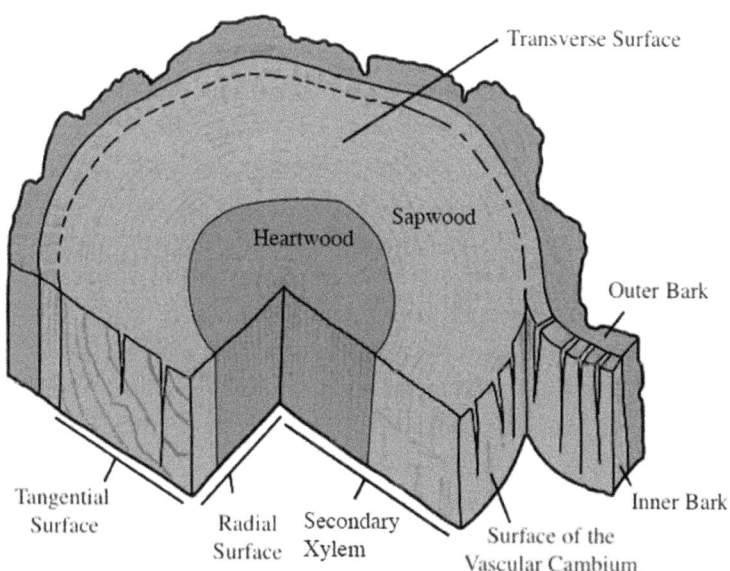

Figure 2 Cross section of a tree stem. Redrawn by author after Raven et al. 2013, 622, fig. 26–12

responsible for the lateral, outward, growth of the tree. Exterior to or within the secondary phloem is the *cork cambium*, which produces additional cork tissues, generally referred to as the *cortex* or *outer bark* (Raven et al. 2013, 615–23; Newsom 2022, 12). To summarize, from the centre of the tree outward, there is the secondary xylem, then the vascular cambium, the secondary phloem (inner bark), the cork cambium, and the cortex (outer bark).

As noted, because the vascular cambium encircles the tree trunk, as it produces new cells, it is producing a concentric ring of secondary xylem (and phloem). Within each ring, the rate of the growth of the secondary xylem cells and the size of the cells being produced changes depending largely on temperature and moisture. For the purposes of our discussion, it is helpful to examine changes in growth in *temperate regions*. The term temperate region refers to areas of the world where there are regular, though not extreme, seasonal fluctuations in temperature and precipitation. Here, conditions are usually optimal for tree growth in the spring or early summer, when there is a good amount of rainfall, sun, warmth, and available nutrients. Under these conditions, cells are produced rapidly. They tend to have thinner walls, and larger central spaces within them, referred to as *lumen*. This thicker section of the ring of secondary xylem is referred to as *earlywood* (Speer 2010, 43). In the periods of the year when conditions are not optimal, growth slows and then may pause entirely. The cells produced during the slow growth period tend to be smaller and denser. This section of the ring is referred to as *latewood* (Speer 2010, 43). The change in density between these two regions produces the visible rings that can be seen in a cross section of a tree trunk – a single *tree-ring* actually represents the full cycle of the production of earlywood and latewood (Fritts 1976, 2; Newsom 2022, 77; Frank et al. 2022, 22). This can be seen in Figure 3. In temperate regions, one tree-ring therefore represents annually changing seasons, and (depending on the species) approximately one calendar year of growth. As the rings build on one another, it is therefore possible to view the regular growth of the tree through the often seasonally produced layers of rings in the secondary xylem. This is the basis for *dendrochronology*, the dating of trees through tree-rings. This is, however, a rather simplified view of the process. A more detailed examination, which slightly complicates this idea of annual tree-rings, will be discussed in Section 5.

Unlike the secondary xylem, outer bark will often slough away from the tree over time, ensuring that the layers of bark remain thin relative to the diameter of the tree, and the thickening secondary xylem (Raven et al. 2013, 620).

Earlywood   Latewood

Tree-ring width

Figure 3 A tree-ring produced in one year in a temperate region. Image by author, adapted from Edvardsson et al. 2021, fig. 3

2.3 The Function of the Secondary Xylem

One of the primary functions of both the secondary xylem and the secondary phloem is to act as a conductive system (Newsom 2022, 13). The secondary phloem is responsible for conducting the products of photosynthetic reactions – nutrients and compounds like glucose. These move from the leaves in the crown of the tree, through to the root system. In addition to keeping the tree anchored, the root system absorbs water and other minerals from the ground. These then move up through the bole, or trunk, of the tree and are conducted through the xylem.

In general, the xylem is responsible for conducting water and minerals within the tree, as well as providing support and food storage (Raven et al. 2013, 615). A more detailed look at how this works helps us to better understand the internal anatomy of the secondary xylem, wood. There are two systems of cells at work in the secondary xylem: the radial, which is horizontally oriented, and the axial, which is vertically oriented. In the radial system, there are cells referred to as *vascular rays*, consisting largely of *radial parenchyma*. *Parenchyma* are active, living cells that can perform different functions, including storage. These rays move the nutrients passing through the secondary phloem from the exterior of the tree to the interior, and move water back from the interior out to the secondary phloem (Raven et al. 2013, 615). There are also *axial parenchyma* cells in the secondary xylem that help move water and nutrients from the roots up to the top of the tree through the trunk, or central bole, and out to the branches and leaves. The phloem, xylem, and roots are, therefore, working together, moving nutrients and water throughout the tree, ensuring that it has what it needs to live. Different species of trees have different types, shapes, and numbers of cells moving these nutrients around, or helping to hold the tree up. In Section 4 when we discuss wood anatomy in more detail, we will explore these concepts further.

Eventually the cells in the oldest, innermost rings at the centre of the tree cease to be active – they are no longer actively moving nutrients. This area continues to provide mechanical support and can store the nutrients already gathered, but has become "functionally dead tissue" (Newsom 2022, 80). This is referred to as the *heartwood* of the tree. The outer layers of the tree that continue to be active are referred to as the *sapwood*. Some of the elements that are typically stored in heartwood include oils, gums, tannins, and resins, which are often called *extractives*. Extractives tend to be quite aromatic and have a darker colour than other nutrients found in wood (Newsom 2022, 80–1). For this reason, heartwood tends to be darker than sapwood – in some cases, dramatically so (as depicted in Figure 2). The extractives within wood can also cause the wood to be denser, harder, and protect it from agents of decay (see Section 3).

2.4 The Chemistry of Wood

In the previous section, I started to discuss the different elements and compounds that might be present within wood, but to understand how wood ages, breaks down, or survives, it is necessary to take a slightly more detailed look at the chemistry of wood. The main components of wood are water, cellulose, hemicellulose, and lignin (Hedges 1989, 112; Rowell et al. 2012, 34). Excluding water, these three latter components make up about 95% of wood. Extractives, the oils, gums, and other elements described in the previous section, make up another 4% of wood, and the final 1% is inorganic ash material (Hedges 1989, 112–13). Cellulose is one of the main components. It is a structural polysaccharide, which means that it consists of molecules of simple sugars. Cellulose accounts for between 40% and 50% of wood, depending on the species (Hedges 1989, 113; Tullus et al. 2010, 101). The structure of cellulose consists of what are referred to as microfibrils. Microfibrils are quite stiff and primarily responsible for the strength of plant cell walls. Hemicellulose is the next major polysaccharide. It accounts for 15–35% of wood. While the types of hemicellulose present are quite variable across wood species, these compounds generally have a branching or spiral structure that is less rigid than cellulose (Hedges 1989, 113–15; Tullus et al. 2010, 101). These compounds therefore contribute to the flexibility of wood structure. Lignins are cross-linked phenolic polymers that make up about 17–35% of wood. These tend to help support the rigidity of wood, which can vary based on the different alcohols present in the lignin. This again varies depending on the species of wood, among other factors (Hedges 1989, 115–16; Tullus et al. 2010, 101).

While this might sound complicated, it is most important to understand how these impact wood cellular structures. The cellulose microfibrils form the framework of the cell wall. This is then surrounded by hemicellulose, which adds some support, but largely allows flexibility as the cell wall expands. The cellulose and hemicellulose parts of the cell are then further supported by lignin, which is the major component found between plant cell walls. There are covalent bonds between lignin and hemicellulose that further help to keep all the cells together and ensure that wood remains stiff and solid (Rowell et al. 2012, 42; Wiedenhoeft 2012, 18). The remaining spaces between these compounds are usually filled with water, helping to fill out the structure. What is really important for archaeologists to understand is that if any one of these elements fails, the cell will collapse. If multiple cells collapse, the wood starts to crumble away. As will be discussed in Section 3, different microorganisms are often attracted to one or more of these three compounds. The breakdown of these different compounds by these microorganisms is the main source of biological wood decay (see Section 3.2).

2.5 Hardwood and Softwood Trees

The information that we have explored so far is applicable to all types of trees that go through secondary growth. As we start to look at tree morphology and wood anatomy in more detail, it will be necessary to differentiate between two main categories of trees and the wood they produce. These are *hardwood* and *softwood* species.

In botanical terms, trees are *spermatophytes*, meaning that they produce seeds. Trees that produce seeds without a covering layer are called *gymnosperms*. Gymnosperms include the softwood trees. Softwood trees tend to have needle-like leaves, and are sometimes referred to as *evergreens*, as they usually retain most of their needles year-round. These trees also often bear cones in which the seeds are produced, giving them the name *conifers* (Shmulsky and Jones 2011, 4). Many people therefore also refer to these types of trees as *coniferous*.

Trees that produce seeds within ovaries are called *angiosperms*. Angiosperms can be divided into *monocots* and *dicots*, and dicots are hardwood trees. Hardwood trees tend to produce broad leaves that drop during the colder seasons in temperate regions. Many people therefore refer to these trees as *deciduous*. The fruiting bodies in which seeds are produced in these types of trees include acorns or pods (Shmulsky and Jones 2011, 4). It should therefore be clear that the terms hardwood and softwood, which will occur throughout the following sections of this Element, refer to different botanical subdivisions. They do not, therefore, necessarily relate to the physical hardness or density of the produced wood – a fact that can cause confusion for non-specialists. On the microscopic scale, the wood anatomy of hardwood and softwood trees is very different. We will return to this discussion in Section 4.

2.6 Further Reading

For an accessible, basic introduction to the science of woody plants and tree growth, see Wiedenhoeft (2012) and Newsom (2022, 73–92). For a more thorough discussion of wood chemistry, see Rowell et al. (2012). For an in-depth, moderately accessible discussion of plant biology, which includes angiosperms and gymnosperms and their different structures, see Raven et al. (2013).

3 The Sources, Survival, and Sample Recovery of Archaeological Wood

We have now discussed how trees grow, and how they produce wood. We have also discussed the basic chemistry of wood. With this background knowledge, we can now move on to considering how wood comes to exist within the archaeological record, and how we can collect it for further analysis. In this section I therefore begin with a discussion of the sources of archaeological wood. This is closely related to how wood decays, and what allows it to survive – or, more accurately, the ways it comes to be preserved. This can help archaeologists consider the likelihood of coming across wooden remnants in their different global and local contexts. I will conclude with some practical suggestions for how to collect wood samples, and how to best ensure that the sample remains intact until they can be assessed by a specialist. As will become apparent, as with so much of archaeology, context is of the utmost importance.

3.1 Sources of Archaeological Wood

Wood can arrive in the archaeological record through a variety of means, both naturally and through human interaction. Because of this, it is important to first distinguish between *cultural wood* and *environmental debris*. Cultural wood was intentionally used by humans. Environmental debris refers to sticks, logs, and other parts of trees that existed or fell naturally. While both may be related to the human–environment relationship, differentiating these remains at a site has obvious implications for interpreting human activities. Some wooden objects, particularly those altered by animals, can look very much like evidence of human manipulation. Consider how animals like beavers or rats can gnaw at wood in ways that make it look like humans have whittled away at it. On the other hand, the use of some mostly or entirely unaltered wooden implements, like a stick used to stoke a fire, can be difficult to differentiate from environmental debris (Newsom 2022, 32). The presence of tool marks, as discussed in Section 6, and the context for wooden objects in and around areas of human activity, can help to clarify these differences. The different possibilities must always be kept in mind, particularly with fragmentary remains.

In terms of the different forms of culturally modified wood, I largely follow Ann Newsom (2022, 36) in her discussion of five potential categories: (1) wooden artifacts and implements; (2) wood in the round; (3) lumber; (4) wood debitage; and (5) charcoal.

Wooden artifacts and implements are usually the easiest of the culturally modified wooden materials to recognize. Simply put, they look like things. This can include large, complex, and complete objects and vehicles, tools, or very small items like pegs and buttons. While these can be found as fragments, or, more rarely, intact, there is often clear evidence that this wood material has been manipulated by human hands.

Wood in the round, roundwood, or round timber are terms used by the timber industry to refer to sections of wood that have undergone little to no processing. They remain largely in their original, cylindrical forms. Natural roundwood, for instance, might be logs or sticks that have simply fallen and collected on a forest floor. Cultural wood in the round, however, might take the form of logs or branches that have been purposefully cut and gathered for human use. The modern timber industry would count poles, piles, or construction logs that have been debarked as round timbers (Senalik and Farber 2021, 6.1). In the archaeological record, roundwood may also appear as poles, architectural implements, or stockpiled firewood.

Lumber is technically "a solid product sawn from a log" (Shmulsky and Jones 2011, 290). Here the term is generally used to describe the boards or timbers (distinguished by their thickness) that will be used to construct architectural features or other objects. In the archaeological record, fragments of processed boards may be found. Additional tool marks or added implements may suggest whether this was stockpiled lumber ready to be used, or pieces that had been joined into larger structures at some point in their use history.

Wood debitage refers to the fragments of wood that are removed from a larger wooden element during the construction process. The presence of tool marks and context is again necessary in order to differentiate these pieces from environmental debris. Unfortunately, these small fragments rarely survive in the archaeological record. On rare occasions, however, this carpentry debris can help to identify woodworking workshops, and provide significant information about tools and the carpentry process. This is particularly helpful from an anthropological point of view, as tool marks are frequently removed from finished products (see Section 6).

The most frequently preserved form of wooden material from across archaeological contexts is fragmentary wood charcoal, or carbonized wood. With the exception of house fires, concentrated areas of wood charcoal are generally seen as reflecting deliberate burning activities. This includes, for instance, wood used in a hearth, oven, or kiln (Asouti and Austin 2005, 3; Pearsall 2015, 41). The form and preservation of charcoal will vary widely. Wood needs to be heated to a certain temperature, usually around 350–800°C, in order to become hard and durable or "charcoal-like" (Pearsall 2015, 42). If wood does not reach these temperatures during burning, some areas may remain softer and susceptible to several agents of decay (see Section 3.2). Carbonized wood is frequently used by archaeologists or paleobotanists for *paleoenvironmental* reconstructions – trying to understand what the ancient environment was like. For instance, charcoal remains can help us to understand what types of trees were available to humans in different regions. Of course, specific conditions need to be met for these types of reconstructions (Chabal et al. 1999; Asouti and Austin 2005; Théry-Parisot et al. 2010).

3.2 The Biological Decay of Archaeological Wood

The various sources of archaeological wood noted in Section 3.1 can be found in some form in many archaeological contexts around the globe. As an organic material, however, there are a number of factors that can impact the survival of archaeological wood. Types of weathering, the general exposure to natural elements such as wind, rain, or sunlight, can cause wooden constructions to break down (Goodell et al. 2020, 3). Animals can take apart wood and use it for nests and other purposes. Humans, of course, may also be responsible for the destruction of wooden objects through such processes as burning or reuse. In this section, however, I focus on some of the most common non-human biological agents that cause decay in archaeological woods, before moving on to the means by which wooden fragments might avoid exposure. Some of the main decay agents are decomposers such as fungi, bacteria, and insects. Environments that are warmer, wetter, and more alkaline, and that have soils with higher carbon and nutrient content, will promote decay at higher rates than those that lack one or more of these factors (Gallagher 2014, 20, Gooddell et al. 2020, 4-5).

3.2.1 Fungi and Wood Decay

As we learned previously in Section 2.4, *The Chemistry of Wood*, the structure of wood cells is primarily made up of cellulose, hemicellulose, and lignin. Different types of fungal rot attack one or more of these components, leading to the collapse of the cell and the decay of the wood. There are three significant forms of wood-destroying fungi: white-, brown-, and soft-rot (Blanchette et al. 1990, 142; Blanchette 1998, 57). We will start with a look at white- and brown-rot. White-rot is caused by a division of fungi called basidiomycetes that tend to attack the lignin within wood. Some species of these fungi will then move on to the cellulose and hemicellulose. The removal of the lignin often causes the wood to take on a bleached, white appearance, as seen in Figure 4 (Blanchette et al. 1990, 143–46; Blanchette 1998, 59). Brown-rot is caused by species of basidiomycetes that tend to prefer to target cellulose and hemicellulose, but can still impact lignin (Goodell et al. 2020, 7). The remaining concentration of lignin causes the wood to appear brown. Brown-rot tends to cause the wood to fracture in a cuboid pattern, as seen in Figure 4 (Blanchette et al. 1990, 151; Blanchette 1998, 58, Gooddell et al. 2020, 7, fig. 1).

For both white- and brown-rot to flourish, the wood needs to be moist, but below total saturation levels. Too much water will create an anaerobic environment in which there is too little oxygen present to permit the fungi to survive (see Section 3.3.2). These types of rot can survive in low-oxygen environments, but not anaerobic conditions (Blanchette et al. 1990, 153). They also tend to prefer a more acidic environment with pH levels of 3.5–5.5. Most species flourish when settled in areas with a temperature of 25–30°C, though some species can survive beyond these ranges (Blanchette et al. 1990, 153).

Soft-rot is generally caused by a division of fungi called ascomycetes and *Fungi imperfecti* that prefer to attack cellulose. Soft-rot is seen as cavities in the cell wall, usually parallel to the cellulose microfibrils (Blanchette et al. 1990, 153–54). Again, due to the remaining lignin, soft rot appears brown, but tends to crack along the grain, and causes the wood to be very soft (Blanchette et al. 1990, 156). In comparison to white- and brown-rot, soft-rot tends to move slower, but is able to survive a greater range of environmental factors. It can withstand even lower oxygen environments, a temperature range from 0°C to 60°C, and a pH range from 3 to 9, so both acidic and alkaline environs (Blanchette et al. 1990, 158–59; Blanchette 1998, 59). Despite the ability of soft-rot to flourish in more diverse environments, it also seems to prefer more nitrogen rich settings. This would be areas of fertile soils or places where there is significant organic decomposition on the ground. It is much less frequently found in above-ground contexts where nitrogen is scarce (Blanchette et al. 1990, 158–59, 2004).

Figure 4 These images show wood suffering from fungal decay. On the left is an example of white-rot, and on the right is an example of brown-rot. Images used with permission from Goodell et al. 2020, figs. 1 and 2.

3.2.2 Bacteria and Wood Decay

Different types of bacteria can impact wood in different ways. For the purposes of this discussion, I will only discuss the three most common types of decay bacteria: erosion, tunneling, and cavitation. Erosion bacteria align with the cellulose microfibrils and erode grooves or troughs into the cell wall, largely degrading the cellulose (Blanchette et al. 1990, 162; Singh, Kim, and Chavan 2019, 848–49). The attack tends to be a bit sporadic, eroding some areas more than others. The affected wood will eventually turn grey or brown and collapse due to the weakening cell structure (Blanchette et al. 1990, 166). Tunneling bacteria tend to move through the wood in a branched system of tunnels, apparently able to degrade both lignin and cellulose in wood (Figure 5; Singh et al. 2019, 860). This tends to turn the material a lighter brown or yellow colour, and breaks down cell cohesion. The remaining wood is therefore soft and sometimes granular (Blanchette et al. 1990, 165–66). Cavitation bacteria tend to form around an area of the cell referred to as the pit border. It often appears as a somewhat elongated cavity (Blanchette et al. 1990, 165).

3.2.3 Insect Damage

Just as with decay due to bacteria, a number of different insects can cause damage to wood in a variety of ways – particularly when building their nests. Some of the most frequent culprits that cause damage to archaeological woods are *xylophagous* insects, those that eat wood. Of those, the most common are

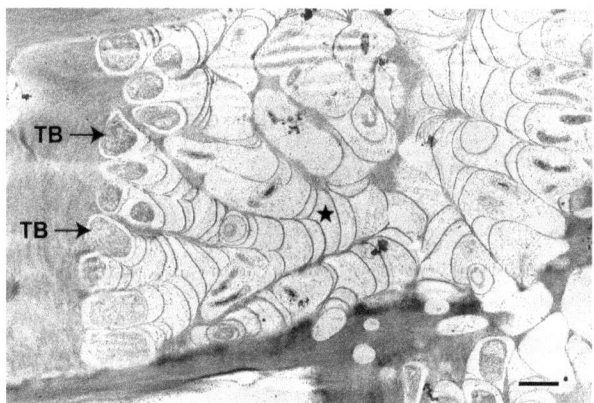

Figure 5 This image shows the impact of tunnelling bacteria moving through a cell wall. TB marks the presence of the Tunnelling Bacteria, while the star marks the beginning of a branching tunnel. Image is reproduced with permission from Singh et al. 2019.

types of beetles (*Coleoptera*) and termites (*Blattodea*) (Pournou 2020, 426). For wood-boring beetles, much of the damage is created by larvae that hatch out of eggs left in cracks in the wood, and proceed to bore tunnels as they eat through the material. These tunnels can range in size from 1 mm to 10 mm in diameter (Blanchette 1998, 62). As the beetles eat through the wood, they digest the polysaccharides. They leave behind a material made of fecal pellets mixed with particles of wood referred to as *frass*. Frass can appear powdery and will often crumble on contact (Blanchette 1998, 62; Pournou 2020, 427). Termite galleries often cause even more decisive damage, creating a full colony within larger wooden structures. While creating networks of internal tunnels, they often leave just a thin (1–2 mm) exterior crust of the structure intact (Reinprecht 2016, 105–6). Insect damage often results in wooden objects with very delicate interior structures. While the tunnels and nests of insects are usually quite obvious, sometimes the extent of the damage is not immediately apparent – particularly when objects have been plastered and painted (see Figure 6).

There are a number of factors that impact an insect's wood selection and their rate of reproduction and decomposition. Some species only attack hardwoods, while others prefer softwoods. Sometimes certain extractives present in the wood will deter insects (and the other forms of decay – see Section 2.3 for more on extractives). For example, extractives called *quinones* are present in teak wood (*Tectona grandis*), which causes it to be repellent to termites (N'Guessan et al. 2023, 200). Two other considerable factors are temperature and moisture. Different species will have different optimal environments, but 20–30°C is

Figure 6 The top image shows the front side of a fragment of archaeological wood covered with plaster and paint. The bottom image shows the other side of the fragment, showing extensive termite tunnels and damage. Almost all the actual wood material is gone. Image by author.

often conducive for larvae production. All insects require a moisture content of at least 10%, but most thrive at slightly or significantly higher moisture levels (Reinprecht 2016, 95; Pournou 2020, 427–28).

3.3 The Survival of Archaeological Wood

Between the destructive habits of animals and humans and decay due to fungi, bacteria, insects, and other elements we have not discussed, it may not be too surprising that wood material does not often survive intact in the archaeological record; nevertheless, there are a number of contexts in which wooden material can survive. In fact, in some global regions, wooden objects can be almost perfectly preserved even millennia after their initial use phase. The best contexts for preservation are of course those that are intolerable for the biological agents just described. These include: dry environments that preserve wood through desiccation; wet environments that preserve wood through anaerobic conditions; and carbonization or mineralization, which transform organic materials to inorganic, rendering them unpalatable to decomposers.

3.3.1 Desiccated Wood

Desiccated wood is generally found in dry, usually desert, environments. The dried wooden objects lack the moisture that decomposing organisms require to survive. If the wooden materials are further protected from other weathering agents, then there is an excellent chance for survival. For instance, if the objects are in dry environments and are also buried in sand or placed in a cave (Newsom 2022, 60). These types of archaeological contexts, however, are somewhat rare. They include, for example, the Great Basin of the United States, Egypt, the Xinjiang region of China, or coastal Peru (Gallagher 2014, 22). Desiccated objects can look remarkably similar to their original state. When wood remains untreated in dry environments, it will dry out, causing the cells to shrink, which may cause some twisting or cracking in the wood, but in many instances this constitutes somewhat minor changes. For these well-preserved objects, anatomical analysis is often possible. For more information on this type of preservation, see Section 7, a discussion of desiccated wood from ancient Egypt in the form of preserved wooden coffins.

3.3.2 Waterlogged Wood

In some contexts, wooden objects in wet environments can also survive. Generally, the wet environment needs to be anaerobic, which means that there is no oxygen. This type of preservation tends to be seen more frequently in areas of heavy sediment or mud. Preservation is also better when the water is quite acidic and when there is little wave activity, which can cause additional erosion (Gallagher 2014, 24). Materials also need to be protected from light, which can cause photodegradation (Newsom 2022, 58). Peat bogs, for example, are often found to be areas of excellent wood preservation. Wood can also be frozen in wet environments, providing another instance of exceptional preservation (Beattie et al. 2000; Gallagher 2014, 24; Newsom 2022, 60).

While the wood remains within these environments, it will often look as if it is well preserved, but submerged wood will undergo some structural and chemical changes; precisely which changes will depend on the species of wood and factors such as the presence or absence of certain oils and extractives. In many instances, water can enter into wood cells, swelling these areas. Eventually, this will cause the relationship between lignin and hemicellulose to break down, weakening the structural integrity of the wood material (see Section 2.4 for an overview of wood chemistry). Over time, the hydrogen and oxygen molecules of water also start to bond to the chemical structures present in wood – particularly those of the hemicellulose, so that water molecules effectively replace the harder crystalline structures (Hoffmann and Jones 1989, 63). While under water, the water molecules are often able to support the remaining lignin structure of the wood, so that it appears stable (Hoffmann and Jones 1989, 63; Johns 2012, 668). Once removed from its wet environment, however, the water that had helped to support the cell structure of the wood dries out. If the wood is removed from the water and allowed to dry rapidly, the cells will therefore collapse and the material will disintegrate (Hoffmann and Jones 1989, 63; Johns 2012, 668). As discussed in Section 3.4, however, if waterlogged wood is gradually dried out, often with additional conservative interventions, it is possible to preserve the material.

3.3.3 Carbonized Wood

As noted earlier (Section 3.1), the most common preservation state for archaeological wood is carbonized wood, or charcoal. When wood is exposed to heat, particularly in low-oxygen environments, it can be transformed into an inorganic, mostly carbon structure (Gallagher 2014, 26). Whether due to a destructive fire event, or due to the use of wood as fuel, only a portion of the original material is likely to survive. Its original state, whether an object or roundwood gathered specifically for a fire, can be difficult to ascertain. The heating of the wood can also cause the material to twist and crack, and break down the chemicals and extractives within wood, but the internal, anatomical structure of the remains is often well preserved. The species of wood used for the charcoal can therefore often be identified through microscopic examination (see Section 4).

3.3.4 Mineralized Wood

The rarest form of wood preservation is mineralized wood. Under some circumstances, when exposed to certain types of minerals, the organic compounds in wood may either leave an imprint in or be replaced by minerals (Gallagher 2014, 25). Different metal oxides or salts such as silicates, calcites, dolomites, ferrous salts, or sulphur compounds, when in contact with wood for an extended period of time, can seep into its cellular structure. Likely starting from the centre of the cell, the lumen, these substances start to fill up the space, and slowly replace the other elements of the cell structure. This can result in a complete replacement of the organic material (Reinprecht 2016, 49–50; Haneca and Deforce 2020, 2). In these instances, usually only very small amounts of the wood are preserved. Examples include remnants of hilts, handles, or shafts of metal weaponry (Haneca and Deforce 2020). Although the remaining samples are very limited, mineralization can preserve the cell structure, permitting anatomical analysis.

3.4 Sample Recovery Procedures for Archaeological Wood

The different contexts described earlier often require different sampling strategies in the field. How and what to sample can also be complicated. While ideally every tiny fragment of wood or charcoal would be assessed, this is usually not practical. The excavators and material specialists should come to agreements about the different variables that need to be taken into account for each project. This will usually involve thinking about the number of samples that could be feasibly assessed in a season, whether there is adequate storage for future analysis, and what types of questions are most vital for the project (D'Alpoim Guedes and Spengler 2014, 77). In terms of preservation, the most important rule is to try to keep the wood in an environment as close as possible to that in which it was found. All remains need to be introduced to new environmental conditions gradually. In the case of waterlogged samples in particular, sample recovery may require specialist oversight and often preservative interventions.

Larger wooden specimens from open-air environments can be collected in situ after the standard excavation procedures, including photography and data recording (Pearsall 2015, 44). This is usually recommended when objects are large and obvious enough to be considered finds, though they may take the form of desiccated, carbonized, or mineralized remains. As long as all of these remains are dry, they are best stored wrapped in acid-free tissue paper, and significant changes in temperature or air moisture should be avoided or introduced gradually. If the remains contain any slight moisture, as is often the case with charcoal, for instance, avoid the use of plastic bags to collect and store samples. Moisture can gather on the inside of the bags and cause the contents to degrade. If the use of plastic bags is unavoidable, lay out the remains or leave the bags open long enough for the moisture to evaporate, and not cause "sweating" on the interior of the bag (Newsom 2022, 68–69).

More commonly, wooden macroremains, particularly charcoal deposits, may be part of archaeological sediments and can be removed through sediment sampling. These samples are then taken to specialists for analysis. There are a number of different sampling methods, and how much should be removed is usually contextually dependent and will follow the approach on site. Often this means removing a certain number of liters of material from across the established excavation grid in order to ensure a representative understanding of the sediment components (D'Alpoim Guedes and Spengler 2014, 78–82). As carbonization is a key means of wood preservation, taking combustion features into account will be important. *Combustion features* refers to concentrated areas of burnt material – like a hearth or oven. Pearsall recommends a blanket approach to this type of sampling (Pearsall 2015, 74–75). This requires that samples are taken from around, above, and below combustion features, instead of just taking samples from within these areas where obvious macrobotanical remains can be found; nevertheless, point sampling from a specific context may be necessary, particularly when storage space or time is a key variable (D'Alpoim Guedes and Spengler 2014, 80; Pearsall 2015, 76; Newsom 2022, 62).

In some instances, the undifferentiated bulk material or samples may be taken back to the lab for separation and analysis by a specialist. In other cases, especially when storage space or transport is a consideration, preliminary processing may be done on site through a selection of different screening systems (Pearsall 2015, 45). If the context is dry, gentle dry sieving is best, allowing wood and charcoal fragments to be separated and collected by hand. A graduated series of mesh sieves should be used for sample collection in this case. This ensures that different sizes of remains will be collected together, which may have significance during analysis. Furthermore, ensuring that a variety of different sizes of samples are gathered will help to avoid biases that can arise from the selection of mesh screens that collect only large or only small pieces (Newsom 2022, 71; Pearsall 2015, 45). In areas of heavy sediment or wetsites, where dry sieving is not possible, water flotation is a common method of recovery.

In flotation, the bulk sample is placed in a container with a screen attached to the base, immersed in water, and agitated (see Figure 7). Some of the material floats to the top, the *light fraction*, and can then be collected with a sieve. Elements that do not float, the *heavy fraction*, sink to the bottom and are caught in the screen, while the remaining dirt and soil passes through. There are a number of variations to this practice, including manual or machine based systems, the additional use of chemicals, and different levels of sieving systems (Pearsall 2015, 46–57). There is some disagreement as to whether wood charcoal can be significantly damaged during flotation. While some studies have found that flotation had little to no impact on the survival of charcoal deposits (Brady 1989), others have found that some of the charcoal disintegrates or breaks apart during flotation (Wright 2005; Fritz and Nesbitt 2014, 117; Pearsall 2015, 43; Newsom 2022, 70–71). As the characteristics of charcoal

Figure 7 A flotation set up with multiple sieving systems used on an excavation. Image by Mark Nesbitt. Public Domain.

vary, it is unsurprising that flotation may impact different sample collections differently. If flotation is to be used, it is therefore advisable to first remove as much of the larger pieces of charcoal or wood before the flotation process. In the cases of wetsite processing, Newsom instead recommends using graduated mesh sieves while passing a gentle stream of water over the samples to separate the wood material from other sediments (Newsom 2022, 70–71, 2006, 185). The finds can then be separated and bagged according to material, with the wooden remnants from wetsites placed in sealed containers with water.

Waterlogged remains need to be kept wet in order to avoid cellular collapse. If there is no wood specialist on site to oversee sample collection, the objects should be moved into wet containers immediately upon removal, and contact with the air should be avoided. Depending on the fragility of the remains, it may be possible to wrap the objects in curation polyfelt fabric, that is wetted along with the object (Newsom 2022, 66). It is best to clean off remaining debris with gentle streams of water, rather than using hard metallic tools (Newsom 2022, 66–67). Of course, it is much preferable to have a conservator or wood specialist on site to handle these samples directly. This should be taken into consideration if waterlogged woods are commonly found in contexts similar to that being excavated.

3.5 Further Reading

For a more in-depth discussion of different recovery methods, as well as a consideration of additional challenges to keep in mind, Pearsall (2015, 35–96) provides an excellent, accessible overview of both sampling strategies and recovery methods. For a discussion of the decay of archaeological woods, Blanchette (1998), Reinprecht (2016), and Gooddell et al. (2020) provide more accessible overviews. D'Alpoim Guedes and Spengler (2014) provide an additional overview of sampling strategies. White and Shelton (2014) provide an additional overview of recovery methods.

4 The Approach to Taxonomic Assessment of Archaeological Wood and Charcoal

Once archaeological wood material is recovered from the field in its various forms, it is then analyzed by specialists. Often this includes analysis by a wood anatomist. In this section, I provide an overview of some of the most common approaches to anatomical analysis that are used to provide (ideally) species-level identifications for wood samples. Technically speaking, this is referred to as a *taxonomic assessment*, as the anatomist is attempting to identify the *taxa* (family, species, etc.) represented by the sample. The purpose of this chapter is to provide archaeologists, curators, or enthusiasts with an understanding of the steps of analysis and some idea of the complexity of wood anatomy. In this way, they can better appreciate the types and sizes of samples that will be most viable for analysis, and have more realistic expectations for what data can be gathered. While this section may provide an introduction for students interested in learning more about this field, it is only meant to cover the basics. Interested parties should look to the further reading section for more advanced and practical guides.

4.1 Primary Data Recording for Wood and Charcoal Analysis

Before taxonomic analysis can begin, some preliminary data about the sample specimens must be recorded. Primary data collection sheets should be completed for any type of wood analysis, providing basic information about the samples that can be used for descriptive or statistical analyses. After receiving the specimen collections from the excavation (see Section 3), the contextual information should be recorded, along with the specimen count numbers for each bag, box, or context. This will allow for total specimen counts to be determined. Total specimen counts and the total number of specimens identified for each context are important for a more accurate understanding of both the ratio and ubiquity of each of the taxa for a total assemblage (Asouti and Austin 2005, 4). For carbonized wood, both total counts and weight or mass of the specimens is usually collected (Asouti and Austin 2005; Newsom 2022, 219). Weights for desiccated woods are not as helpful and not usually collected unless particularly required for some additional reason, often related to conservative treatments (Newsom 2022, 219). While different wood specialists working in different global regions, dealing with different sample sizes, and answering different questions will often carry out different statistical analyses on their data, recording the total or absolute counts for each context is almost always the first step.

It is important to consider which specimens will be identified. Often, some degree of subsampling is required. For carbonized wood analysis especially, specimens are often in the thousands or tens of thousands. This scale is frequently not feasible for a study, though in some cases this is completed in order to ensure an accurate understanding of the environment. One way that the sampling scale is reduced is by setting a minimum size of the samples to investigate. Asouti and Austin (2005, 7) have noted that samples less than 4 mm may not yield the anatomical features required for an identification. Other scholars suggest that it may be necessary to set the minimum at 2 mm, if preservation is limited (Théry-Parisot et al. 2010, 143). Using a graphing approach referred to as a *species-saturation curve* can help to ensure a representative number of samples is reached for a particular stratigraphic level, when attempting to reconstruct the paleoenvironment (Asouti and Austin 2005, 6–7; Newsom 2022, 233).

The additional information that is recorded as part of the primary data collection sheet will often vary depending on research question and context. Some common elements include morphometric data such as the measurements of specimens, the presence of pith or bark, the type of specimen (worked wood, debitage, roundwood, etc.), the presence of any tool marks or decoration and additional construction and carpentry data (including initial processing), and any additional information about the wood's preservation state (Newsom 2022, 224–31). Growth-ring curvature in charcoal and growth-ring width in wood specimens can also provide information about fuel collection and environmental data, among others (Newsom 2022, 229–31).

Once this basic information has been recorded, then the sample can be further processed for taxonomic assessment. Once an identification has been reached, this should be added to the general datasheet. A sample data sheet that I have used in my analysis of desiccated wood has been included in the supplemental materials for this Element. A separate recording sheet is used for anatomical features for each taxon. Most wood anatomists use the IAWA hardwood and softwood data sheets for this purpose (see Section 4.5). While macroscopic features such as colour, texture, or grain are useful for modern wood analysis (Ruffinatto and Crivellaro 2019), identification of archaeological woods focuses on microscopic traits (Wheeler and Baas 1998, 243–45; Newsom 2022, 171).

4.2 Sample Preparation for Degraded Wood

When first approaching taxonomic identification of wood, it is necessary to remember that wood anatomy is three-dimensional. As discussed in Section 2, certain cells are transporting nutrients up and down a tree, others are moving them laterally, and the organization of these different cells is different for each species of tree. In fact, these elements can vary between sample specimens as well, as shall be discussed next. As noted in Section 2.3, the axial system makes up the vertically oriented cellular elements, while the horizontal elements are called the ray or radial system (Newsom 2022, 95). The variability in both systems needs to be assessed in order to confidently suggest an identification for a wood sample. In order to evaluate these systems, a wood specialist needs to be able to view three planes of reference: the transverse, radial, and tangential.

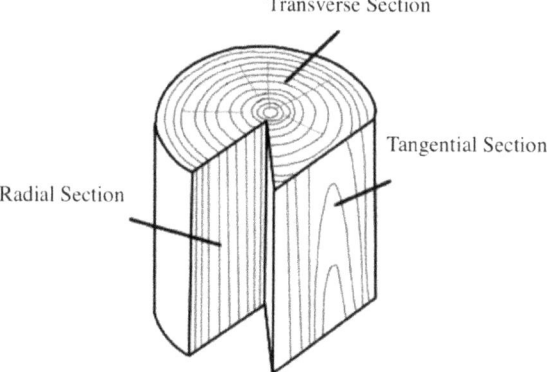

Figure 8 The planes of reference used to assess wood anatomy. Redrawn by author after de Geus et al. (2020, fig. 2).

Figure 8 provides an illustration of the three planes of reference. The transverse section, or cross section, is visible by cutting through the tree trunk at a 90-degree angle. The radial and tangential are oriented longitudinally along the trunk of the tree. If a section of trunk can be considered a circle, with the top face being the transverse section, cutting into this circle at the radius would reveal the radial section, and cutting into the circle at a tangent would reveal the tangential section. When preparing a sample, these planes must be exposed, either by fracturing along these planes, or, more commonly, by preparing a thin section for each of the planes. Fracturing refers to controlled breaking of the wood to expose each plane. When fracturing wood, the exposed plane will not be entirely flat – it will have topography. To assess fractured planes, the sample therefore has to be viewed by approaches that can be refocused on different heights of the topography to get a clear picture of the whole surface. For our purposes, this generally means using either reflected light microscopy (RLM) or scanning electron microscopy (SEM). The other approach is to cut very, very thin, flat slices of wood from each plane. These are then prepared on slides for transmitted light microscopy (TLM), which is the most common approach.

Because sections must be prepared for each of the planes, the samples that must be removed from wooden objects need to have a three-dimensional area. In ideal circumstances, when the aesthetic qualities of the wood are not an issue, a sample of 5 mm^3 should be plenty of material to confidently provide thin sections for each plane. Of course, when working with worked objects or artifacts, this is generally not possible. In these cases, samples of approximately 2–3 mm^3 are considered standard (Cartwright et al. 2011, 51; Cartwright 2019, 2). Very thin sections, even if quite long, are not ideal, as they are unlikely to permit a view of the transverse section; however, it is still sometimes possible to gain good information from smaller samples, particularly with high-powered machinery such as SEMs. These require less intensive sectioning, but are often prohibitively expensive. They are also too large and require too clean and controlled an environment to take into the field.

When selecting areas on artifacts to sample, avoid areas of degradation due to fungi, bacteria, or insect damage, where the cellular structure of the wood may have been impacted. Taking samples from near additive materials such as plaster or paint should also be avoided. This helps to maintain the integrity of the object, but also increases the likelihood of a positive identification. Added materials can seep into the wood and have an impact on the ability to view the internal anatomy, making identification more difficult or impossible. Some preservative materials, such as Paraloid B72, also adhere to the cellular structure of the wood, complicating anatomical identification (Altobelli et al. 2023). If an object has been treated extensively with these types of consolidants, it might not be possible to provide an identification. Where possible, samples can be taken from inside joints or cracks, making less of an impact on the object, and often remaining free of additive materials. It is best to work with a curator when these objects are in museums to come to an agreement about the size and location of samples.

Unfortunately, exposed wood on the edges of objects does not usually sit on a perfect plane of reference. The exposed areas of wood also often have at least a finely frayed surface that obscures details. This means that samples almost always need to be taken from objects. If it is not possible to obtain a sample, it may be feasible to provide partial data through the use of reflected-light microscopy, though it may not be possible to reach species-level identifications at this magnification or view (Newsom 2022, 157). If good planes of reference are exposed, another alternative is to remove sections directly from the object, rather than taking a sample to section (Newsom 2022, 158). Finally, recent work has demonstrated the promise of micro-computer tomography (micro-CT) scans that would allow wood anatomists to study reference planes non-destructively (Pearl et al. 2020, 31; Dierickx et al. 2024). For the moment, there remain too many limitations to this approach to replace wood sampling for archaeological materials, but no doubt this will change in the near future.

When preparing thin sections of degraded wood, the specialist first ascertains the orientation of the fragment – which means they determine where the planes of reference are located. Often this is apparent due to the fracture patterns in the wood. When the samples are very small, however, sometimes an initial inspection with a low-powered stereoscope microscope is necessary to verify the orientation. If the piece is encrusted or covered over with other materials, these obstructions must be removed. The thin sections need to be cut exactly along the planes of reference. Even a slightly oblique view often appears distorted and makes the assessment of anatomical features very difficult. A thin section is then removed from each plane, a process referred to as *sectioning*, and mounted on a slide.

If the wood sample is very hard and cannot easily be sliced, it must be softened. Sometimes, just adding a drop or two of water is enough to soften wood that is slightly too hard or curling; however, it may be necessary to boil the sample in water or soak it in 70% ethyl alcohol. Of course, the analyst must be confident that the sample is preserved well enough to sustain such treatment (Hoadley 1990, 83; Newsom 2022, 156). If it is too delicate, a larger piece could be embedded in material such as paraffin wax, and then sections would be removed with a freeze or sledge microtome, a machine that is capable of cutting very thin slices from materials (Newsom 2022, 156).

Before sectioning, glass slides should be labelled and prepared with an aqueous solution. This can take the form of a small drop of water or glycerol. While water may be sufficient for well-preserved desiccated wood that can be quickly identified, glycerin 50% aqueous solution (glycerol), ensures the sample remains moist for longer, which is necessary for extended viewing under a microscope (Newsom 2022, 154). Once the slide is prepared, sectioning can commence.

There are a number of ways that thin sections can be removed, which can be dependent on personal preference, the preservation of the sample, and the significance of the potential data. In each case, however, the blade used to section must be very thin and very sharp. I usually prepare sections by hand using a double-sided razor blade with medical tape applied over one side. Bruce Hoadley (1990, 72) suggests that you could also break these in half with pliers to make them safer, while Ann Newsom prefers the use of a "high-profile disposable microtome blade but without the handle" (2022, 155). The double-sided razor blades are effective though with obvious safety risks, but are much cheaper than microtome blades. The blade is then used to slice off a paper-thin section along the plane. This section is then placed on the prepared slide and covered over with a coverslip, now ready to be examined under a transmitted light microscope.

4.3 Sample Preparation for Carbonized Wood

Preparing carbonized wood samples for taxonomic analysis requires a different procedure from that used for degraded or desiccated wood. Carbonized wood samples are much more brittle and so should not be sliced into sections. This can crush the sample, or cause the cellular structure to collapse (Hoadley 1990, 192;

Newsom 2022, 160). Instead, the samples should be fractured so that the planes of reference are exposed. This is usually done by assessing the longitudinal direction of the wood grain, and then breaking the sample perpendicular to the grain by hand to first expose the transverse section (Newsom 2022, 159). When analysis of this plane is complete, the sample can then be broken down further into the remaining longitudinal planes (Hoadley 1990, 192; Dussol et al. 2016, 58; Newsom 2022, 159). The samples can then be viewed under a reflected light microscope.

4.4 Technology for Taxonomic Assessment

The majority of degraded wood samples are analyzed using a transmitted light, compound microscope. To identify all the anatomical features, it is often necessary to view details between 40x and 600x magnification, though some of the more minute details may require up to 1000x magnification. Different brands of microscopes that reach these magnifications are usually sufficient for analysis; however, some of the more advanced capabilities such as polarizing or fluorescence may be helpful to view features such as crystals (Newsom 2022, 165). Carbonized samples are usually assessed with a reflected light stereomicroscope. These microscopes are lower in magnification, reaching around 90x magnification, or up to around 230x with additional lenses and oculars (Newsom 2022, 166). When these forms of analysis are found to be insufficient for species-level identification, higher powered instruments should be used.

There are additional approaches that are possible with a larger budget, and sometimes necessary for very fragile or significant samples. Both degraded and carbonized samples can be analyzed using an SEM, for instance. In these cases, the wood samples can either be sliced or fractured, as an SEM can be used to study differential topography (see Section 4.2). Depending on the type of SEM, additional sample preparation may be required. In some cases, for instance, the sample must be coated with a very thin layer of gold prior to analysis in order to create a more reflective surface. Sometimes, with variable pressure or environmental scanning electron microscopy, however, these additional steps are not required (Arbuckle MacLeod et al. 2021, 97–98; Newsom 2022, 162). SEMs allow for higher magnification and resolution analysis of samples, and are particularly useful for very small samples that are difficult to section.

4.5 The Basics of Taxonomic Assessment

Once it is possible to view the anatomy of a sample, the anatomist records which features are visible. Each species of tree has a unique anatomy. Generally, the presence or absence of different features allows the wood anatomists to first differentiate between hardwood and softwood species. After this basic division, the presence or absence of different features are used to further divide between possibilities related to families of different trees, until ideally reaching a species-level identification. In the following discussion, I provide an overview of some of the basic elements that can be seen in the different planes of reference. This is once more a simplified discussion in order to demonstrate what types of information wood anatomists are examining; however, the International Association of Wood Anatomists (IAWA) committee has created two fundamental works that provide a detailed overview of the different features of wood anatomy. These are divided into those that are particularly diagnostic for hardwood (1989) and softwood (2004) species (see also Wheeler and Baas 1998).

Usually, wood anatomists begin by looking at the transverse section (TS) to document the presence or absence of elements within the axial system. This should provide the basic distinction between hardwood and softwood. As a reminder, the terms *hardwood* and *softwood* are botanical subdivisions, and do not necessarily reflect the physical hardness of wood (see Section 2.5). From an evolutionary perspective, softwoods are less advanced, and their anatomy tends to be less complicated (Newsom 2022, 95). In softwoods, a type of cell called a *tracheid* provides both conduction and support, while in hardwoods, a tubular cell referred to as a *vessel* performs the primary water conduction (see Figures 9 and 11; Newsom 2022, 96). So, if vessels are absent, the wood sample generally comes from a softwood tree. Once this distinction has been made, documentation of the other features helps to further subdivide down to an ideally species-level identification. This usually means viewing the anatomy from the three different planes of reference.

4.5.1 Softwood Anatomy

Figure 9 provides a three-dimensional illustration of the anatomy of an example softwood species, demonstrating features that are visible in specific planes. An example of how the different features look in micrographs (photographs taken using a microscope) is provided in Figure 10. In general, anatomists are interested in assessing what is present or absent in the axial and ray systems, and how these systems interact (see Section 4.2). For softwoods, the axial system is largely composed of tracheids. These elongated cells are arranged in rows, reflecting their formation by the vascular cambium (Newsom 2022, 99). In the transverse section, these rows can appear more or less dense depending on whether they represent latewood or earlywood growth. The extent of and transition between these growth periods, the growth increments, are variables

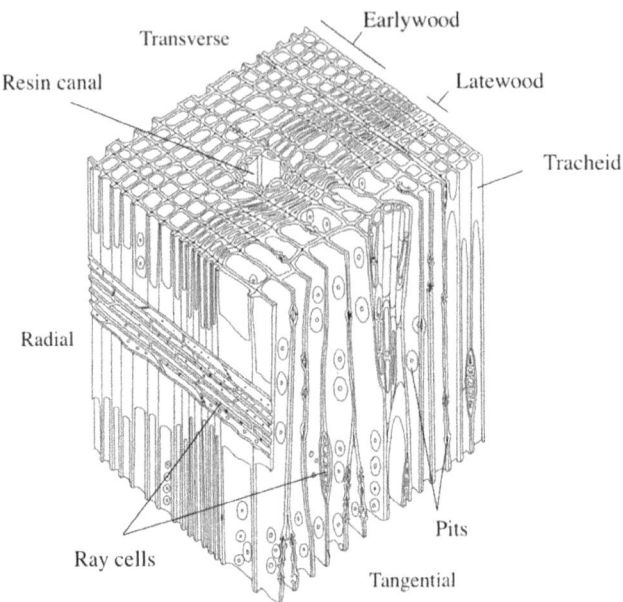

Figure 9 A three-dimensional view of features typically seen in the anatomy of softwood species. Redrawn by author after Arzola-Villegas et al. (2023, fig. 1).

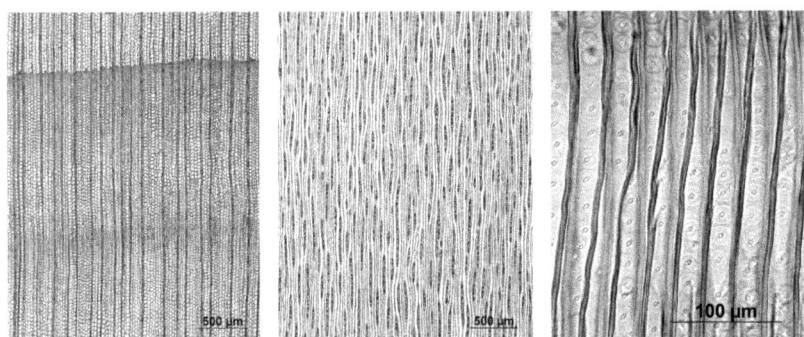

Figure 10 This figure shows the micrographs for each plane of reference for the softwood *Cedrus libani*, taken by a transmitted light microscope. The image on the left shows the transverse section, the middle shows the tangential section, and the right shows the radial section. Images courtesy of Michael Risse, and available on InsideWood.

that can assist with identification (IAWA Committee 2004, 16–18; Newsom 2022, 100). The basic distinctions that an anatomist looks for in this case are for whether the growth-ring boundary is distinct or indistinct, and whether the transition from early- to latewood was abrupt or gradual. For instance, in the transverse section in Figure 10, the growth-ring boundary is distinct, and the transition is gradual. To review the basics of tree growth, see Section 2.2.

The ray system in softwoods is primarily composed of radial parenchyma cells, though radial tracheids can be found within some species as well. Parenchyma are brick-like cells that facilitate the movement of nutrients, and may retain some of their contents at the time of analysis (Newsom 2022, 100). There may also be resin canals in some softwood species, which can move both axially and radially. These move resins or secondary plant products throughout the tree structure (IAWA Committee 2004, 58). While the presence of these canal systems is normal in some species of softwood trees, in others they are produced as a defense response to a type of wounding – and are generally called *traumatic resin canals* (Nagy et al. 2000; IAWA Committee 2004, 60). The presence or absence of these different types of canals is diagnostic. In the tangential section in Figure 10, single rows of ray parenchyma cells stacked on top of each other are shown in between the tracheids. In this case, some of the parenchyma cells appear darker, like dark bubbles, due to remaining cell contents. Since these rows are only one-cell thick, these rays are called unicellular. There are no resin canals.

The different types of cells often have cavities in both their side and end walls, which are referred to as pits, helping to move cell contents around. The size, arrangements, and borders of these pits are diagnostic. The pits and shape of the area created by intersecting walls of tracheid and ray parenchyma cells, referred to as cross-field pitting, are other elements commonly assessed for softwoods (IAWA Committee 2004, 51; Newsom 2022, 102). In the radial section in Figure 10, the scalloped edges of bordered pits are visible. This is a particularly diagnostic feature associated with species of cedar trees such as *Cedrus libani*.

4.5.2 Hardwood Anatomy

Figure 11 provides a three-dimensional illustration of the anatomy of an example hardwood species. An example of how the different features look in micrographs is provided in Figure 12. As noted earlier, hardwood trees have a more complicated anatomy than softwoods. Axial tracheids are quite rare in hardwoods, and thick-walled fibres instead take on the main structural role in the axial system. Fibres surround the often wide vessels that appear as large pores in the transverse section. The size of the pore, or the width of the lumina of vessels, and their frequency and the pattern of their arrangement, are usually some of the first features recorded when assessing hardwoods (IAWA Committee 1989, 236–44; Newsom 2022, 108). In the transverse section in Figure 12, for instance, this wood is considered diffuse porous.

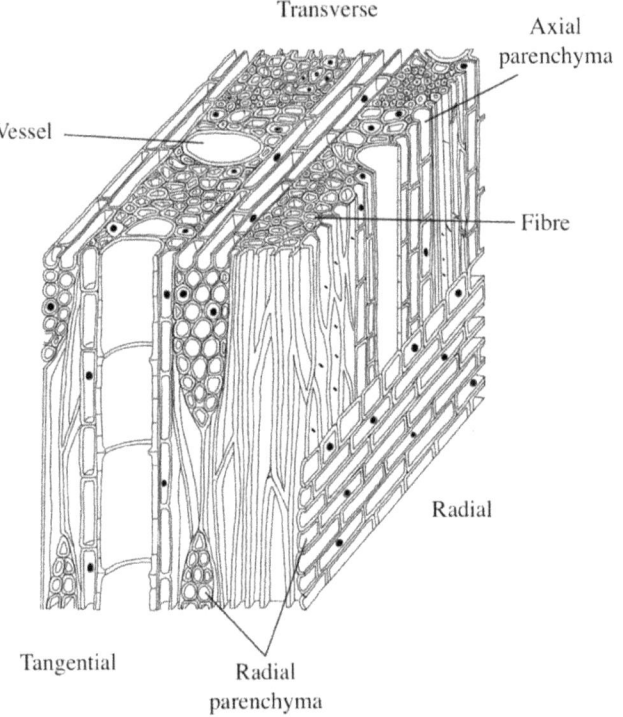

Figure 11 A three-dimensional view of features typically seen in the anatomy of hardwood species. Redrawn by author after Fahn (1990).

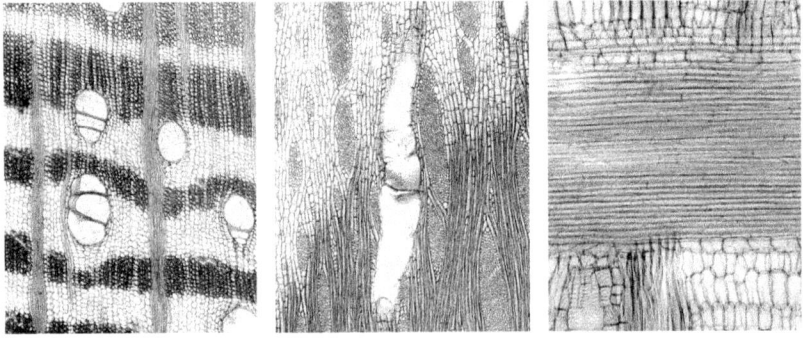

Figure 12 This figure shows the micrographs for each plane of reference for the hardwood species, *Ficus sycomorus*, taken by a transmitted light microscope. The image on the left shows the transverse section, the middle shows the tangential section, and the right shows the radial section. Images by Pieter Baas, available on InsideWood.

In hardwoods, parenchyma cells are common in both the axial and radial systems. In the axial system, the patterns created by the parenchyma, particularly their relative position to vessels, are diagnostic, and can be viewed in both the transverse and radial sections (IAWA Committee 1989, 270–81). In Figure 12, the alternating bands of fibers and parenchyma are visible in the transverse section. While in softwoods, rays are usually unicellular, or one cell thick (see Figure 10), in hardwoods, radial parenchyma width can vary across and within species, and can be assessed in either of the longitudinal sections. In Figure 12, in the tangential section, we can see that the rays are larger, commonly 4–10 cells wide, with a few even wider than that. The way that the parenchyma cells stack on top of each other, whether they are all procumbent or some are upright, is another feature best viewed in the radial sections (IAWA Committee 1989, 288–90). Rays with procumbent and border upright cells can be seen in the radial section in Figure 12.

As with the softwoods, the shapes and arrangement of pits in the various cells can again be diagnostic. With hardwoods, however, it is often the ray-vessel and intervessel pitting that is most useful (IAWA Committee 1989, 250–55). In addition, the shape of the perforations in between vessels, referred to as *perforation plates*, can be helpful for species identification as well (IAWA Committee 1989, 246–49).

For a non-specialist, all these details about anatomy may seem a bit overwhelming. What is really important to understand is simply that there are many different variations in wood anatomy, and many of these variations are best viewed in specific planes. This is why having access to all three planes is vital for a confident identification – and why a three-dimensional sample usually needs to be taken for assessment.

4.5.3 Wood Identification Keys and Atlases

As the different elements of the anatomy are viewed, the wood anatomist records these features. These are recorded on a separate and specific datasheet than the general sample datasheet discussed earlier (Section 4.1). The IAWA has provided datasheets for both hardwood and softwood species, which can be accessed on the website InsideWood (InsideWood 2018). These keys include long lists of numbered features that relate back to the published lists of microscopic features previously noted (IAWA Committee 1989, 2004). The wood anatomist can tick what is present or conspicuously absent. While technically these can be used for both desiccated and carbonized wood, Ann Newsom has developed a charcoal recording form that takes into account different observable features (Newsom 2022, 169, Appendix D). Once the initial list of features is recorded, the wood anatomist checks these features against different types of anatomical keys.

There are many different types of keys that relate to different approaches to arriving at an identification. Dichotomous keys present a series of contrasting, paired choices. The different choices take the anatomist down a branching path eventually arriving at an identification (Wheeler and Baas 1998, 253). This system is more useful when there is a limited selection of possibilities (Wheeler and Baas 1998, 253; Newsom 2022, 171). Synoptic keys focus instead on creating lists of taxa that include specific features (Wheeler and Baas 1998, 253). While these types of keys are still helpful, particularly when working in the field with limited access to internet, it is much more common today to at least begin narrowing down possibilities using a multiple entry key connected to a digital database.

The standard database for this purpose is currently the InsideWood Database (insidewood.lib.ncsu.edu), which is structured around the IAWA lists of microscopic features (Wheeler 2011). The anatomist inputs the visible features corresponding to those listed on the IAWA datasheets. As the numbers of present or absent features are input, the database searches for taxa that meet these parameters. Ultimately, this provides a short list of species that exhibit the selected features. At this point, the wood anatomist should look at each of the possible species and check additional features against what is present in their sample. InsideWood often provides images of the different planes of reference along with the lists of features (as seen in Figures 10 and 12), to help researchers check similarities. Final verification will require checking features listed in additional atlases, and ideally checking against a reference collection of vouchered (known and identified) physical wood samples as well (Newsom 2022, 172–73). As Wheeler and colleagues have stressed, a database can only check the species that have been included within it, and so completing final checks to verify identifications with additional resources is vital (Wheeler and Baas 1998, 258; Wheeler 2011).

Wood anatomical atlases are usually related to a specific geographic region. As these are specific to a limited context, the included selection can already help to narrow in on a possible identification. These publications often include a discussion of vocabulary, identification keys, and then individual species descriptions and photographs (for example, Crivellaro et al. 2013).

4.5.4 Challenges and Variables for Taxonomic Assessment

Recognizing all the different elements within wood anatomy is challenging. This is because some features that are associated with a single species will always be present or absent, while some may show up in certain samples, and not in others; some features always present the same way, while others can appear slightly or very differently. This can be due to a number of reasons – root, branch, and trunk wood can differ, wood from trees that grow in certain microclimates can differ, and wood from trees growing on different terrain can differ. The ways that trees and their cell structures vary, due to their stage of maturity, their function, or variations due to environmental differences are robust areas of study referred to as functional and ecological wood anatomy (Wheeler and Baas 1998, 258–59; Schweingruber 2007; Newsom 2022, 123). Desiccation or waterlogging can also cause cells to shrink or swell, particularly causing challenges with size variables used for identifying archaeological woods (Newsom 2022, 101). If the sample suffered from any factors of decay or destruction (see Section 3.2), these will also have a significant impact on the ability of the anatomist to identify features. For example, in Figure 13, an insect has eaten through the centre of the wood sample, obscuring anatomical details.

Because there can be so much variation in wood, it is important that enough specimens are examined before suggesting which features are particularly diagnostic for each species within keys (Wheeler and Baas 1998, 247). If the

Figure 13 This is a micrograph taken by SEM, and shows an insect tunnel moving through the centre of a sample. Image by Caroline Arbuckle MacLeod and Caroline R. Cartwright.

features differ significantly from what is presented in published keys, it can cause problems or delays for interpretation. Most wood anatomists focus on specific regions. Over time it becomes easier to recognize the common species from that specific context, as well as the different ways variables can be expressed. This is why establishing a personal reference collection of wood specimens is so helpful for wood anatomists, as they are more likely to be able to witness a wider range of possible variations than the much more limited published examples.

A final vital note to remember, which is constantly reiterated by wood anatomists, is that sometimes the sample will not be adequate to provide an identification (Fritz and Nesbitt 2014, 118). The required anatomical features may not be present within the small sample, or the wood may be too fragmentary or damaged. In these cases, it may be possible to suggest whether the sample is of hardwood or softwood, or provide a family-level identification, or at least a description of what elements are visible. This information can still be helpful for understanding the context or material (Wheeler and Baas 1998, 251; Newsom 2022, 221). It is vital, however, that the wood anatomist does not feel pressured to provide a "best guess" identification. These types of actions can, and often do, cause errors to enter into the archaeological record, and can take decades to correct. Excavators and curators should instead understand that sometimes identifications are simply not possible, no matter the skill or experience of the anatomist.

4.6 Further Reading

For an accessible overview of the identification procedure, focusing on modern woods, see Hoadley (1990). For a more detailed overview of the sampling and analysis process, with additional discussion of potential practical challenges see Wheeler and Baas (1998) and Newsom (2022, 153–215). There are also a number of discussions of charcoal analysis and potential challenges for archaeological interpretations (Asouti and Austin 2005; Théry-Parisot et al. 2010). For a more in-depth, but still introductory, discussion of anatomical features visible in wood, I recommend Wheeler and Baas (1998) or Newsom (2022, 93–152). Look to the IAWA publications for the fundamental works describing the many microscopic anatomical features found within hardwood (IAWA Committee 1989) and softwood species (IAWA Committee 2004). For an overview of functional and ecological variation with additional bibliography, see Newsom (2022, 124–52). For a more detailed examination of different ways that the environment can impact plant structure, see Schweingruber (2007). For an overview of the InsideWood Database and additional notes about its function, Elisabeth Wheeler and other members of the IAWA team have provided resources (Wheeler 2011; Wheeler et al. 2020).

5 Dendrochronology and Tree-Ring Research in Archaeology

Dendrochronology, or the science of dating tree-rings, was first established as a science by the astronomer Andrew E. Douglass (Douglass 1920; Kaennel and Schweingruber 1995, 91). Based on his premise of *cross-dating* (see Section 5.1), he was ultimately able to establish a 1229-year-long tree-ring-based chronology for New Mexico that dated back to 700 CE (Douglass 1935; Tegel et al. 2022, 2). This approach has since been developed and replicated in many areas of the world. Some of the dendrochronologies date back as far as 14,300 BP (Kaiser et al. 2012; Lageard 2022; Tegel et al. 2022). The precision of dendrochronology, being able to date objects to a specific calendar year was, and remains, impressive. Such resolution is rarely achievable using scientific methods. While there are a number of challenges for this method, it remains an excellent tool for archaeologists. Tree-ring analysis has evolved considerably since Douglass' approach. It is now a multidisciplinary subject that is of interest to many scientific fields that focus on answering historic and prehistoric environmental questions. In the following discussion, I focus on the basics of this approach and its use for establishing chronologies in archaeology, before touching on topics such as dendroecology. The purpose of this section is to elucidate potentials and challenges of dendrochronology for archaeologists and the interested public. Readers should look to the further reading guide (Section 5.5) for more detailed and specialized discussions.

5.1 The Basics of Dendrochronology

In Section 2.2, we learned about the production of the secondary xylem, or, wood. As you may recall, the cells of the secondary xylem are produced as concentric rings by the vascular cambium. The size of the produced cells changes depending on environmental conditions such as rainfall and sunlight. When conditions are optimal, the cells are produced rapidly, and are larger with thinner walls (see Figure 3). The ring of these cells is referred to as earlywood (or spring wood). When looking at a cross section of wood, this area of cells can look lighter in colour. When conditions are less than optimal, cell growth slows, and the cells are smaller and denser. The ring of these cells is referred to as latewood (or summer wood). In a cross section, the latewood areas can look darker. Where seasonal cycles are regular, such as in temperate regions, the combination of earlywood and latewood generally represents a calendar year of growth (Frank et al. 2022, 22). In the cross section of a tree-trunk, the change in density between earlywood and latewood, causing that lighter and darker appearance, usually creates readily visible growth rings, or, tree-rings (see Figures 3 and 15). The goal of dendrochronological analysis is to assign a specific calendar year to a specific tree-ring on a piece of wood. If this is done with modern, living trees, you should ideally be able to assign a calendar year to every annual tree-ring from a core taken from it. Since you know that the outermost ring will date to the year the tree was cut or sampled, you should be able to assign a known calendar year to the rest of the rings as well. Of course, in practice this is a bit more complicated.

Each year the amount of sunlight, rainfall, and other environmental conditions are different. This means that the width of the earlywood and latewood rings of trees will be different each year too. Because the same species of tree growing in the same region will be similarly impacted by the environment, in theory, they will share the same tree-ring patterns or *signatures* (Baillie 1995, 16; Tegel et al. 2022, 8). Tree-ring signatures from living trees and those found in wooden products made from the same species of tree from the same region can be compared and aligned. When you know the calendar dates represented by the tree-rings in the living tree, you can then assign calendar years to those in the related object. This process is referred to as *cross-dating* (Douglass 1941; Fritts 1976, 2; Kuniholm 2001, 35). By overlapping cross-dated trees and wooden objects, a chronology can be extended back from a living tree to historic or prehistoric objects. This can produce a very reliable, absolute, long chronology, as presented in Figure 14. Once cross-dating has been achieved, the dates should be verified through comparisons with other regional tree-ring chronologies and other patterns of tree growth from the region. This is a process referred to as replication (Speer 2010, 4; Frank et al. 2022, 31). Once a long chronology has been established, it can serve as a reference. When new wooden objects are discovered, if their signatures can be matched up to the reference, they can also be cross-dated. This can then potentially provide a precise felling date for the wood used for the object, or at least a *terminus post quem* – the earliest possible date for the creation of the object (see Section 5.4). It should be stressed that as only trees of the same species from the same region can be cross-dated, the species of the archaeological woods must also be identified for the dendrochronological information to be of use (Tegel et al. 2022, 6).

5.2 Sampling and Recording Tree-Rings

Generally, when working with archaeological woods, the most effective method for recording tree-rings is by viewing a cross section of the wood. On structural or roundwood found on excavations it may be possible to saw through the wood to

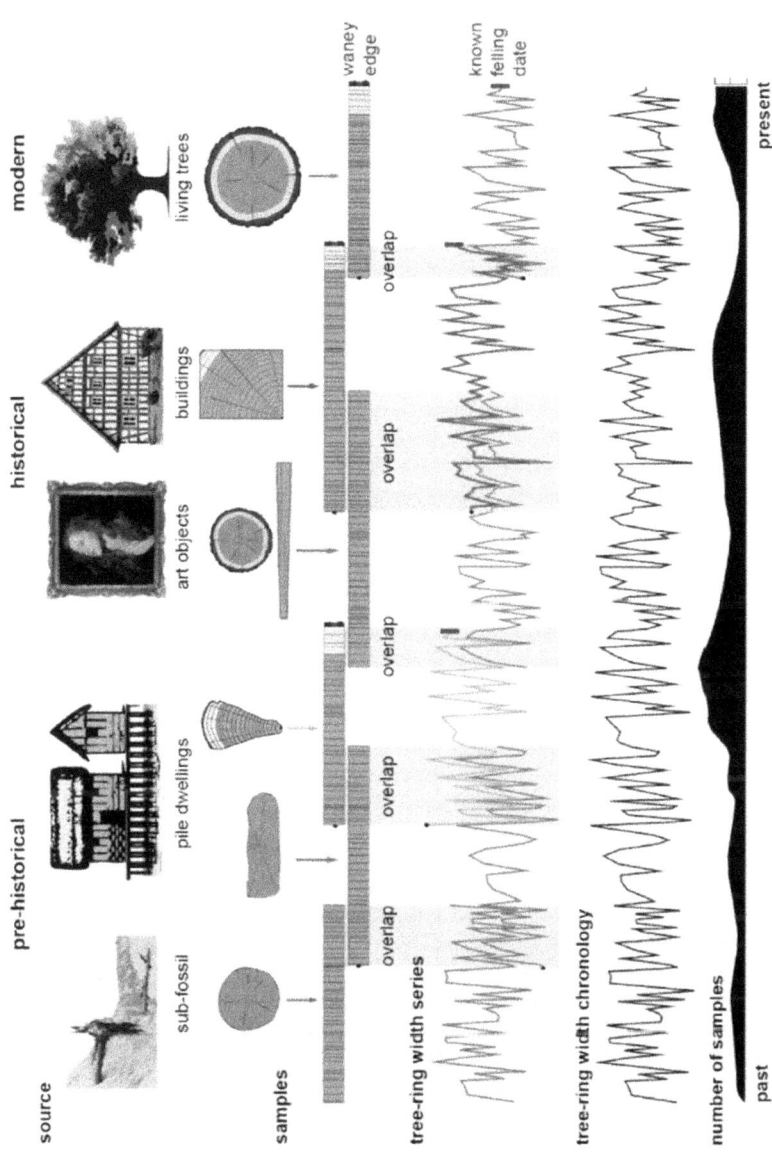

Figure 14 Illustration of the cross-dating process. Image from Tegel et al. 2022, figure 2, used with permission of the authors.

form a cross section. Of course, this should only be done after documentation and where the aesthetic qualities of the object are not significant. On more sensitive objects, a core section can be drilled with a tool called an increment borer. Sometimes though, if the grain is visible, it may be possible to simply clarify the grain by shaving the surface of the wood (Baillie 1995, 18; Tegel et al. 2022, 6; Lageard 2022, 4–5). In recent years, there have also been promising advances with the use of X-ray computed tomography to view tree-rings as well (Bill et al. 2012; Martinez-Garcia et al. 2021; Lageard 2022, 6; Tegel et al. 2022, 7). Ideally, these different analyses would include a view of what is referred to as the *full tree-ring sequence*. This means being able to view the rings from the centre pith of the tree through to the bark, or the layer just below the bark, referred to as the *waney edge*, the last ring produced before felling (see Figure 15; Kuniholm 2001, 37; Tegel et al. 2022, 6). A full tree-ring sequence therefore includes every growth-ring that was originally present in the cross section of the tree. There are a number of complications related to taking samples that are beyond the limits of this discussion, but suffice it to say, these samples should be taken by an experienced dendrochronologist whenever possible (Lageard 2022, 4–5). If not possible, the person taking the sample should make it clear where on the object the sample was from, and if any bark or the waney edge was present on the object. They must also ensure that the sample contains as complete a tree-ring sequence as possible, usually with at least 50 visible rings (see Section 5.4).

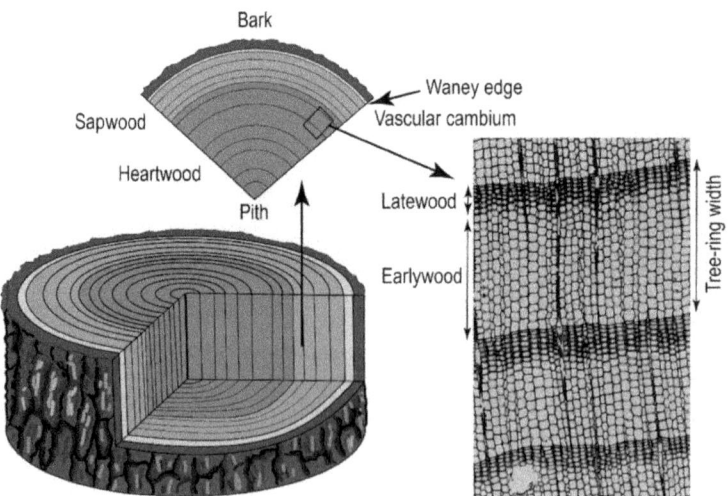

Figure 15 Illustration of the waney edge, and the relationship of earlywood, latewood, and tree-ring growth. Image used with permission from Edvardsson et al. 2021, fig. 3.

If the waney edge is accessible, it may be possible to assign an exact calendar year to the felling date of the tree used to create the object. If not, it may only be feasible to suggest the earliest possible felling date, a *terminus post quem* (Kuniholm 2001, 37; Tegel et al. 2022, 10). Where the sapwood of the sample does not survive, it may be possible to estimate the number of years missing, and provide an approximate felling date. For some species we know that sapwood becomes heartwood (see Section 2.3) over a fairly standard period of time in a specific region. Therefore, if it is clear that the heartwood rings of the tree are complete, the number of rings that could possibly be missing from the sapwood can be estimated, providing an approximate *terminus post quem* (Baillie 1995, 23; Edvardsson et al. 2021, 10; Lageard 2022, 8).

Once the form of the sample is ascertained, the rings themselves can be counted and measured, which produces a tree-ring series. In the past this was done manually with limited materials (Kuniholm 2001, 37). Today, however, it is more common and usually more precise to use additional technology to count and measure the rings. There are a number of approaches used for this. One method is using a stereomicroscope connected to a device called a linear encoding stage (Frank et al. 2022, 24). The researcher might also use semi-automatic measuring tables and digital recording programs such as Coo Recorder that record measurements from images (Maxwell and Larsson 2021; Tegel et al. 2022, 8). Whichever technique is used to measure the tree-ring widths, these measurements are then transformed into a graph, skeleton plots, or other types of data (Baillie 1995, 20; Lageard 2022, 6). These can then be compared to other tree-ring series. If the dendrochronologist is creating a reference series from living trees, it is best to take multiple samples from the same tree, and then from different trees in the same region for comparison. If working from archaeological materials, if at all possible, multiple samples should be taken from different areas of the object to create comparable tree-ring series (Edvardsson 2021, 6). During this comparison, the researcher should account for variables that may be present in a single sample, such as missing rings, particularly thin rings, partial rings, variations due to the size or age of a tree, and more (Baillie 1995, 20; Frank et al. 2022, 30–31, 35–40; Tegel et al. 2022, 8). Comparing these different series and accounting for these anomalies helps researchers determine the average tree-ring parameters for this species in this area. Once tree-chronologies have been established for different global regions, new archaeological finds can be compared to these *master chronologies* (Kaennel and Schweingruber 1995, 217).

5.3 Fixed and Floating Chronologies

There are a number of variables that complicate a researcher's ability to establish a fixed, absolute, master chronology using dendrochronology. The trees need to be long-lived and available in all historic periods being examined. There also needs to be enough standard variation in the tree-rings in order for cross-dating to be possible (Baillie 1995, 25). The tree-ring chronology then needs to extend to living trees. With living trees, we can be sure that the outermost layer of the sample dates to the present year. This therefore provides a chronological anchor (Baillie 1995, 25). Chronologies that can be extended to the present provide what is referred to as a *fixed* chronology, because it is anchored to a reliable and specific known year-date.

Sometimes, however, there are breaks in these chronologies. We may discover a number of wood samples from the archaeological record that all share the same tree-ring signature somewhere in their series. By overlapping the tree-ring series of these samples, we may even be able to create a long series spanning thousands of years; however, if we cannot connect this series to that from a living forest community, for which we know for certain the calendar year of the outermost rings, we will lack a chronological anchor. The remaining data can therefore tell us that the wood used for these different objects is contemporary, but it cannot be connected to a specific calendar date (Kaennel and Schweingruber 1995, 146). This is what is referred to as a *floating* chronology. These are still useful as they demonstrate relationships between objects. Moreover, if the approximate date of one of the objects is known, this can help provide at least an estimate for the felling date for the trees used for the other objects. Ideally, however, these series will continue to be extended until they are connected to a series based on a living tree. At this time the chronology will become fixed and an absolute date can be suggested for the objects connected to the series.

5.4 Selected Challenges and Potential Solutions for Assessing Tree-Rings in Archaeology

The following discussion touches on some of the most common pitfalls and potential related solutions that arise during archaeological analyses. In order to use tree-rings to date a wooden object, the rings must be associated with annual tree growth, and a reference tree-ring chronology must first be established for the specific wood species in a specific growth region. This brings up a number of challenges. Many species growing in temperate regions, where there are significant, seasonal fluctuations, create more-or-less annual growth rings that can be counted and measured to produce a series. Unfortunately, trees growing in tropical areas, or places that do not have regular, annual seasonal changes, will usually not produce clear, annual growth rings. For many of these species, basic cross-dating is therefore not possible, and these trees cannot be used for standard approaches to dendrochronology; however, new advances to the means by which tree-rings or seasonal growth can be assessed is rapidly expanding the list of viable species (Pearl et al. 2020; Lageard 2022, 2). For instance, while changing tree-ring width is the most obvious visual indicator of the seasonal shifts used to measure tree-rings, there are also changes to wood density, anatomy, and the isotopic composition of the wood cells. These approaches can sometimes be used as alternatives to standard annual growth rings to document changes in tree-rings or growth over time (Schweingruber 1993; Frank et al. 2022, 23; Lageard 2022, 6).

Another issue is being able to identify the provenance of archaeological wooden materials. Again, only wood samples from the same region can be cross-dated. For cultures that had ready access to a variety of trees, they would often use the species that were locally available. In these cases, it may not be particularly difficult to determine where to start looking for potential reference chronologies for cross-dating. Throughout history, however, wood has been imported for use by different cultures, sometimes from vast distances. In these cases, there may also be multiple possible areas of import. The researcher must therefore first identify the specific region from which the timber originated before they can begin attempting to cross-date the sample. For example, cedar wood was imported into Egypt from west Asia from very early in its history. While researchers have good reason to believe that a significant proportion of the cedar trees came from Lebanon, multiple regions are possible (Pulak 2001, 24; Arbuckle MacLeod 2024). Without additional data, it will be difficult to begin to search for cross-dating possibilities. On the other hand, however, sometimes it is possible for a researcher to match the tree-ring series of an object to a reference chronology. In this case, it may not only be possible to date the sample, but also to suggest the provenance of the timber. This is referred to as *dendroprovenancing* (Edvardsson et al. 2021, 11–12). Sometimes scientists can also perform analyses of stable isotopes in the sample to identify a possible provenance, and then look for comparable tree-ring series. A combination of both approaches can help ensure the reliability and precision of the results (Van Ham-Meert and Daly 2023). Finally, many scientists are working to make it easier to find potential reference chronologies. Global tree-ring chronology data is becoming increasingly accessible, thanks especially to large databases such as the International Tree Ring Data Bank (ITRDB), with additional work on database management being completed each year (Pearl et al. 2020). As this discipline continues to develop, hopefully creating and sharing reference chronologies will expand the viable tree-ring communities as well.

Frustratingly, after figuring out the provenance of wood, and finding a potential reference chronology in a database, the tree-ring sequence from an archaeological sample may still not cross-date. This may be due to unique circumstances that affected a small selection of trees from that area, or specific stress events to individual trees (Baillie 1995, 52). To combat this issue, when dendrochronologists are first establishing tree-ring chronologies they will include "multiple cores per tree, multiple trees per site, and multiple sites per region" specifically to attempt to account for these types of issues and noise variance (Frank et al. 2022, 41). In addition, dendrochronologists and dendroecologists are often interested in trees that have been impacted by diverse environmental factors such as flooding or insect outbreaks. They will therefore often include these specimens in their analysis, as well as a secondary group to serve as a control site (Frank et al. 2022, 33; Lageard 2022, 4). Some of the different variations and anomalies that impact the average tree-ring parameters for that region are therefore recorded.

A certain number of tree-rings also need to be preserved within the object in order for enough of the sequence to be tested to ensure that the signatures do truly cross-date. A minimum of 50 rings has traditionally been required, though 100 or more is often seen as being more reliable (Baillie 1995, 12; Pearl et al. 2020, 926). In some cases, it may be possible to use shorter tree-ring series, but the researcher would have to be confident that there is enough of a unique signature to make cross-dating possible. Of course, they would also have to acknowledge a larger possible margin for error (Edvardsson et al. 2021, 5–6). In the cases where a short-ring series is considered unreliable for dating, it may still reveal valuable archaeological information. Short-ring series can, for instance, provide data on wood fuel exploitation strategies and changes in woodworking technology (Blondel et al. 2018; Pearl et al. 2020, 927).

A number of additional possible issues may occur when attempting to assess the age of wood that does not display the full tree-ring sequence. As noted earlier (Section 5.2), it can be feasible to estimate the possible years that are not represented due to missing sapwood rings; however, if none of the sapwood remains at all, it is possible to badly over or underestimate how much of the heartwood is missing. This can cause a misinterpretation of the dates of objects and corresponding construction phases (Baillie 1995, 62–64). This is an issue that arises during the interpretation of the data, and must be kept in mind when working with dendrochronological samples.

Final interpretative issues that relate to tree-rings and archaeology are the "relic wood" and "old wood" problems (though the term "Old Wood Problem" has been used to relate to both phenomena). The first part of the issue is that even if a wood specimen is dated accurately using dendrochronology, this tells us only the felling date of the tree – and does not necessarily reveal the use date by the culture in question. In Michael B. Schiffer's (1986, 20) discussion of the use of Ironwood (*Olneya tesota*) in the Sonoran Desert, he notes that deadwood could lay quite well preserved for millennia before being used for purposes such as firewood. This is therefore the use of *relic wood* for uses or activities that occur significantly after the felling date. Wood that has been reworked or reused from older constructions provides a similar challenge. This problem is further compounded when the wood is radiocarbon dated. If the lifespan of a tree is considerable, the rings at the centre of the tree could have a much older radiocarbon date than the outermost rings. This is referred to as the *Old Wood Problem* or effect (Warner 1990, 160). Schiffer therefore suggests that the lifespan of a tree should be taken into consideration when providing the radiocarbon dates for a specimen (1986, 25 see also section 5.5). While these dates can therefore comfortably support a *terminus post quem*, additional contextual information should be incorporated where possible to ensure that the human activities under study correlate with the felling date of the tree (Cook and Comstock 2014).

Dendrochronology has considerable promise for providing accurate dates for archaeological wooden objects; nevertheless, this short selection of potential challenges should make it clear that both creating tree-ring sequences and extending dendrochronological data to archaeological interpretations should be done with care. Both require the careful work of experts who are familiar with the significant number of possible variables at play.

5.5 Dendrochronology and Radiocarbon Dating

Radiocarbon dating is based on the analysis of carbon isotopes. Carbon 12 and carbon 13 isotopes are stable, but carbon 14, or radiocarbon is not. It breaks down at a known rate (a half-life of about 5,700 years). By assessing the amount of carbon 14 that remains in carbon-containing materials, such as wood, an age range can be provided (Taylor 2017, 689). Although this theory has been proven effective overall, unfortunately, on a global scale, there is some variation in carbon 14 activity. This means that the carbon 14 ages often do not align exactly with a calendar date (Taylor 2017, 693). As tree-rings contain carbon, and are often created annually, each ring has the potential to provide an accurately dated sample of the changing radiocarbon levels during different historic and prehistoric periods in different global regions (Pearson et al. 2022, 574). A series of tree-ring dates and their associated radiocarbon dates can be taken at specific time intervals in a process called *wiggle matching* (Bronk Ramsey et al. 2001,

381). In this way, dendrochronology can be used to create localized calibration curves to help the carbon 14 ages to provide more precise calendar dates (Pearl et al. 2020, 931; Pearson et al. 2022, 575–76). Wiggle matching has also been used to provide more accurate dating estimates for wood samples connected to floating chronologies (Galimberti et al. 2004).

5.6 Dendroecology

The premise of dendrochronology is based on the fact that there are environmental shifts from year to year that impact the width and composition of tree-rings; the study of tree-rings therefore also provides insights into shifts in the ancient environment. The related discipline of dendroecology includes the various subfields that use tree-rings to consider ecological challenges (Kaennel and Schweingruber 1995, 95). The number of subfields is still growing, but currently includes dendrochemistry, dendroclimatology, dendrogeomorphology, dendrohydrology, dendroglaciology, dendrovolcanology, and more (Lageard 2022, 9). Tree-ring analysis can therefore help us understand historic fluctuations in pollution, changes in the climate, floods and droughts, glacier movements, and the variable ways that volcanic eruptions have impacted the environment (Schweingruber 1993, 2007; Lageard 2022, 9–15). As with tree-ring dating, the analysis of changes in wood anatomy, density, and isotopes has been crucial to these various fields.

5.7 Further Reading

For an accessible overview of dendrochronology and other tree-ring research for archaeology, including different environmental analyses and possible variables see Frank et al. (2022) and Lageard (2022). For an overview with a focus on the history of dendrochronology in Europe, see Tegel et al. (2022). For an extensive glossary of dendrochronological terms, see Kaennel and Schweingruber (1995). Although slightly out of date, one of the fundamental works on the approach to dendrochronology remains Schweingruber (1988). For a discussion of the integration of dendrochronology and radiocarbon dating, see Pearson et al. (2022). For a discussion of the different challenges that arise with dendrochronology, and issues with interpretation in the cultural heritage sector, see Edvardsson et al. (2021).

6 Assessing Ancient Woodworking

Globally throughout history, woodworking has been one of the most common methods of constructing objects and structures. The relatively soft material is easily formed, and evidence of hominin modification of wood has been found that dates back to as early as 476,000 years ago (Barham et al. 2023). Craftspeople in different regions of the world have developed unique and often ingenious construction techniques. Incredibly though, the basic selection of hand tool types is remarkably universal. This makes the study of archaeological evidence for woodworking slightly more straightforward. When assessing evidence for woodworking, there are several methods used to first view and record the technical elements of production. These elements include initial processing or conversion methods, as well as types of tools and joining techniques. Additional approaches, such as ethnoarchaeology and experimental archaeology, can then be used to help interpret the dynamic processes that ancient craftspeople used to fashion these artefacts. In the following discussion, I provide an introduction to these different methods for recording and interpreting evidence of woodworking.

6.1 Initial Wood Seasoning and Processing

When wood is first cut from a tree, it is not generally considered ideal for construction, with specific exceptions (Bates 2013, 33). A living tree contains a considerable amount of water. As wood dries out the cells shrink. If an object has been made from fresh wood, or *green* wood, it is likely to split or warp as it dries due to the cells shrinking. It will also be more susceptible to rot (Hoadley 2000, 87). Instead, wood should be left to slowly dry out or *season* until the moisture content in the wood is relatively consistent with the average relative humidity of its intended location (Hoadley 2000, 87). In other words, the moisture content in the wood should be about the same as the room in which it is kept. Only after seasoning can the wood be worked into an object or construction – and even then, changes in the atmosphere will likely alter the wood slightly. Seasoning can take a considerable amount of time depending on the global region and time of year – from a few months to a few years. Wood can be left to season as roundwood, or can be cut into rough planks, and left to dry out before being further processed. When assessing the steps of production and the length of time it takes to create an object, this initial lengthy step should be taken into consideration (see also the discussion of *chaîne opératoire* in Section 6.3).

Once wood has been seasoned it can be used for additional projects. Sometimes logs are used largely as unaltered roundwood, as, for instance, structural or cultural poles, but usually it is further reduced and used for other projects. This may include carving the piece into a specific shape, but often wood was reduced into planks of lumber. Transforming logs into boards or planks that could be used by a carpenter or joiner to construct other objects is a process referred to as *conversion* (Bates 2013, 32). There are several choices that a woodworker can make at this point that reveal different construction knowledge or priorities. As illustrated in Figure 16, woodworkers can remove planks of wood from the trunk, or bole, of the tree, cutting tangentially through the wood from the top to the bottom, using a "through and through" conversion method (Bates 2013, 33). This produces lumber referred to as *plainsawn* in hardwoods and *flat-grained* in softwoods (Newsom 2022, 41). Alternatively, woodworkers can split the trunk into quarters, and then further reduce these sections into planks cut along the radius. This produces lumber referred to as *quartersawn* in hardwoods and *edge-grained* in softwoods (Newsom 2022, 41).

These different forms of log reduction have benefits and drawbacks during construction. Plainsawn lumber ensures that the least amount of wood is wasted, and is often the most straightforward method (Bates 2013, 33); however, even with well-seasoned wood, fluctuations in heat and moisture over time will cause the material to swell and shrink. There are different forms of movement in the different orientation of wood cells, but tangential shrinkage is more significant than radial (Hoadley 2000, 74–75). This means that plainsawn wood is more susceptible to warping, particularly cupping, in which the edges of the wood raise above the centre (see Figure 17). While quartersawn wood is less likely to

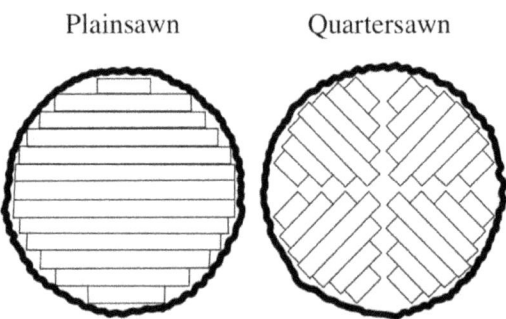

Figure 16 Plainsawn and Quartersawn log reduction methods. Image by author.

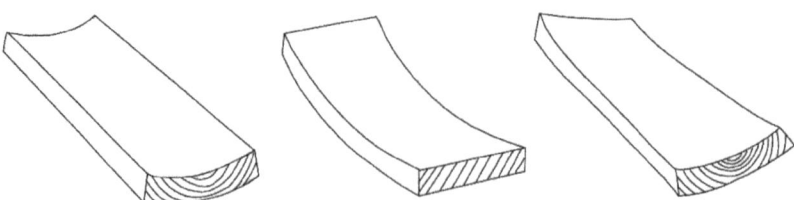

Figure 17 A selection of different forms of wood warping. From left to right, there is an illustration of cupping, bowing, and twisting. Image by author after WOOD 2021.

warp, wood material must be wasted in the conversion process (Bates 2013, 33). In wooden objects, the conversion method can usually be viewed in the end-grain or cross section of objects. This may help to reveal either knowledge of wood movement, or suggest selection priorities (see Section 7 for examples).

6.2 Evidence for Carpentry Practices in the Archaeological Record

Tool marks refers to the marks that are left on wood after the material has been worked with tools. These can provide excellent insights into both the available technology of a culture and specific techniques and movements used by a carpenter or a community. Unfortunately for archaeologists, elaborate wooden products have usually been smoothed over, removing any of these marks in the final stages of construction; nevertheless, these can still be viewed on incomplete objects, between joints, on woodworking debris, and on materials like structural wood or roughly finished objects where the removal of tool marks was considered unnecessary (see examples in Section 7). Of course, this requires a high level of preservation, and so is usually reserved for desiccated or waterlogged woods.

While interpreting tool marks can be challenging, it is made much more straightforward when the cultural *toolkit* is accessible. This refers to the full tool assemblage available for woodworkers in different regions at different times. This varies, of course, between different cultures and time periods; however, up until the industrial revolution and the advent of modern machinery, there were a selection of fundamental woodworking tools that are frequently found throughout history, many of which are still used by carpenters around the world today (Williams 2008, 107).

In exceptionally well-preserved cases, additional construction information may be available from complete wooden objects. The techniques used for joining wood, for instance, can reveal significant information about the knowledge and practice of a community, which communities are in contact, and how approaches change over time due to technical, social, and other developments.

6.2.1 The Woodworking Toolkit

Archaeological evidence for the woodworking toolkit can be somewhat elusive depending on the context. Prehistoric toolkits are generally reconstructed from surviving tools or through visible tool marks on the wooden remains. Rob Sands, for instance, notes that while extant tools are rarely found in Bronze or Iron Age Scottish crannogs, the tool marks at his sites suggested the use of axes, knives, gouges, chisels, borers, and awls to work wood (Sands 1997, 57–59). Communities whose living descendants continue to practice traditional woodworking can also, of course, provide essential information. A number of North American Northwest Coast Indigenous artists are noted by Hilary Stewart in her reconstruction of the cedar working tradition, which was dominated by hammers, wedges, adzes, and chisels. Many parts of these tools were made of stone, and more recently, metal, but other organic materials such as wood, bone, and antler serve as reminders of the types of evidence that might not survive (Stewart 1995, 29–35).

Information from some ancient communities can be quite robust. There are significant numbers of preserved tools as well as worked wooden objects from ancient Egypt, for example. In addition, this culture also painted illustrations of woodworkers and woodworking workshops on tomb walls (see Figure 18), or carved wooden models of these scenes to be placed in tombs. Literary and economic texts provide even further evidence for the practices of ancient Egyptian carpenters (Gale et al. 2000; Arbuckle 2018, 120–47). Evidence from ancient Rome is likewise significant and detailed (Ulrich 2007). This level of insight, however, is quite rare. Given the differential preservation of evidence, it is often necessary to use cross-cultural comparisons to assess toolkits and manufacturing techniques (Maragoudaki 2019). If a region's toolkit is not yet known, it may be useful to consider tools that are common to many toolkits to help see what is or what is not present in the region under study. The following provides a general overview of the types of tools that are frequently found in ancient toolkits, and remain significant elements of today's traditional hand tools.

Figure 19 shows a collection of tools that would make up the basic toolkit of a carpenter or joiner in the 1800s. Many of these tools, or variations, were used throughout the ancient world as well. Woodworkers would often have a number of tools for measuring and marking up the plan of their project on the wood. This might include rulers with culturally determined units of measurements, and different systems of levels that were often based on a hanging weight called a bob or plumb line and bob. A selection of compasses and squares for measuring out angles, and painted or chalked strings or lines for marking out designs would also be useful in the planning stages (Ulrich 2007, 22; Bates 2013, 1–5).

Rougher cutting tools helped with the initial shaping of the pieces that might be joined together for more complex projects. These included axes and hatchets, which are among the oldest types of woodworking tools (Ulrich 2007, 22), and a variety of saws. The shape of the axe head, and the size, shape, and different direction of the teeth of the saws may differ based on the intended function of the tool, or the technological knowledge of the culture (Bates 2013, 5–7).

After the initial shaping, a variety of sizes and shapes of adzes, chisels, awls, knives, and borers or augers could be used for further rough shaping, or detailed

Figure 18 On a wall painting from the tomb of Rekhmire at Thebes in Egypt, carpenters work with a selection of tools. In the top register, from left to right, a carpenter smooths a carved furniture leg with a rubbing stone. In the centre, three men use rubbing stones to smooth a lotus-shaped wooden column. On the right, the carpenter saws through a piece of wood using a pull-saw. In the bottom register, from left to right, a carpenter strikes a chisel with a mallet. Centre-left, four men work with chisels and adzes while working on a wooden shrine. Centre-right, one man carves with a chisel, while the other works with a pull-saw. On the right, two men work a bow-drill together to drill a hole into a wooden bed. Image from the Metropolitan Museum of Art 35.101.1, Rogers Fund, 1935 (Creative Commons license).

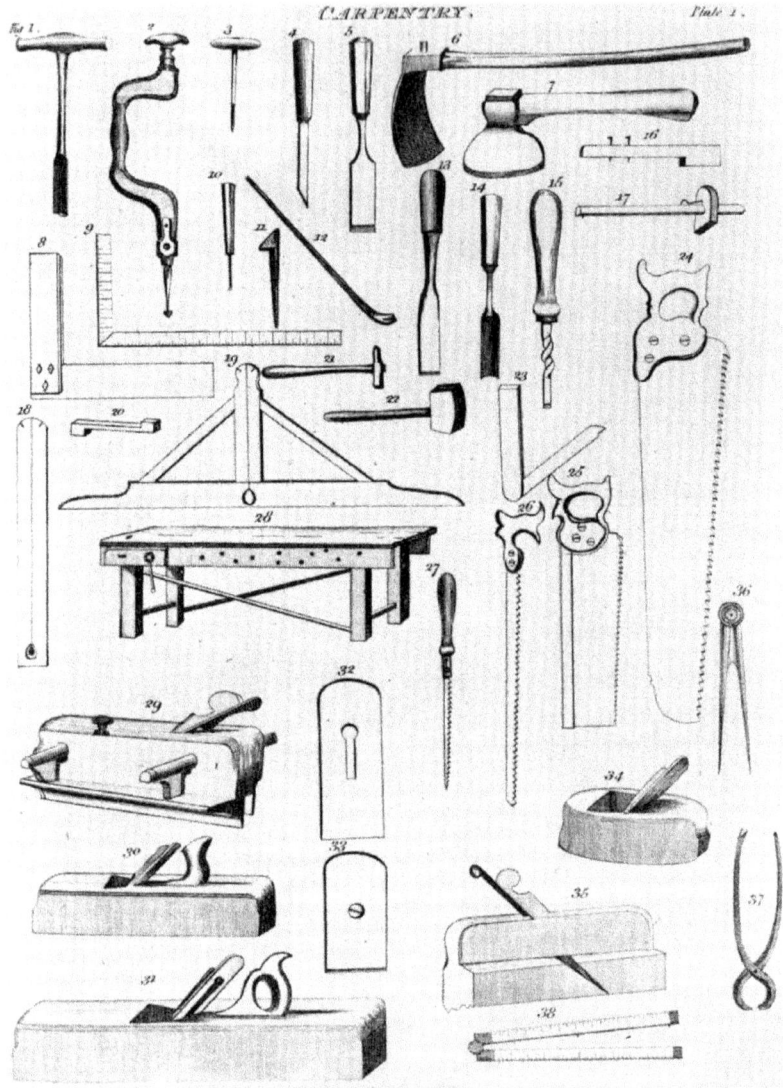

Figure 19 A selection of important tools used by a carpenter and joiner. 1. Auger, 2. Stock and bit drill, 3. Gimlet, 4. Mortise chisel, 5. Firmer chisel, 6. Adze, 7. Axe, 8. Square, 9. Square, 10. Awl, 11. Hookpin, 12. Crowbar, 13. Socket chisel, 14. Gouge, 15. Turnscrew, 16. Gauge, 17. Gauge, 18. Plumb rule, 19. Level, 20. Sidehook, 21. Hammer, 22. Mallet, 23. Bevel, 24. Saw, 25. Tenon saw, 26. Compass saw, 27. Keyhole saw, 28. Workbench, 29. Plow plane, 30. Jack plane, 31. Trying plane, 32. Plane blade, 33. Plane blade, 35. Molding plane, 36. Compass, 37. Pincers, 38. Rule. Image from Martin 1813, Plate 1.

finishing (Ulrich 2007, 41; Bates 2013, 7–9). Additional tools such as the plane, which seems to have first emerged in the first century BCE (Ulrich 2007, 41), might be used to help smooth a surface. A *bow-drill* was common for quickly creating holes. Bow drills consist of a *bit*, around which a thong or string was looped and then attached to a stick or bow. As the bow is moved back and forth, the motion causes the bit to spin, and pressure applied to the top of the bit pushes it into the wood (the bow-drill is being used in the bottom right of Figure 18). A heavy duty version of this tool, called the *strap drill*, was used by the ancient Romans to drill deeper, larger holes in heavy timbers (Ulrich 2007, 33).

Files, rasps, gouges, or seemingly less specialized tools such as stones or shells could be used to create either very smooth, or specifically textured surfaces during the final stages of production. Throughout the construction process, different types of hammers and mallets, clamps, and wedges were also often utilized (Ulrich 2007, 13). There are, of course, additional specialized tools found throughout cultural assemblages, though the variety are too great to be discussed here. As noted earlier, the finer finishing processes and details would erase the rougher tool marks, making them more difficult to identify archaeologically. Where they are left, however, they record the presence of these different tools, and may reveal more about the woodworkers' choices and organization.

6.2.2 Assessing Tool Marks

From a primary perspective, tool marks can help provide insight into the tools that the woodworker used to complete the construction of objects, and sometimes which details were completed with specific tools. The most common identifiable tool marks belong to one of two types of tools: hewing tools and sawing tools. Hewing tools are generally those used for chopping, such as axes, adzes, or chisels. Those used for sawing are of course saws. Sawing is sometimes specially referred to as lumbering (Williams 2008, 106). An individual tool mark produced by a single strike of a bladed, hewing tool is referred to as a *facet* (Sands 1997, 11; Newsom 2022, 48). The edge of a facet, where the tool has stopped, is referred to as a *stop mark* or a *jam curve* (see Figure 20). These can provide information about the width and profile of the tool used in its creation (Sands 1997, 11; Brunning and Watson 2010, 21). For saws, the tool mark is referred to as a *kerf mark* or *kerf chatter*. The term *kerf* refers to the space or void removed from the wood by the saw teeth as the tool moves through the material. It is the shoulder of that void that is the kerf mark (Williams 2008, 108).

Figure 20 This image shows examples of tool marks. On the left is a worked piece of wood with chisel facets, with the arrow indicating the stop mark. On the right, saw kerf marks can be seen down the face of a piece of wood working debris. The arrow indicates the edge of a single kerf mark. Image by author.

While this basic information can suggest what type of tool was used, a close analysis of the details in these marks can provide additional insights into the construction process. On the long axis of a facet, the ridges and grooves created by knicks or damage to the blade can create a characteristic signature. These signatures can demonstrate associations between worked pieces of wood (Sands 1997, 4). Basically, if the same signature can be tracked on closely associated pieces of wood, it can be demonstrated that the same tool was used to work both pieces. As Sands (1997) has demonstrated, this can then provide insights into the organization of work. Other types of observations regarding the symmetry, smoothness, or direction of tool marks can also suggest, for example, the skill of the carpenter or the level of challenge posed by the hardness of the timber in question (see Sections 6.3, 6.4, and 7 for examples).

6.2.3 Assessing Joining Methods

As mentioned previously, in exceptionally well-preserved instances it may also be possible to assess the joining methods used in archaeological contexts. These are the ways that carpenters join two (or more) pieces of wood together. While there are a multitude of possible joining techniques, many of which are culturally specific, only a selection of the most common will be discussed presently. It should also be noted that different workshops may have different terms for these joints, and the following are those used by wood specialist Geoffrey Killen (Gale et al. 2000, 358–66; Killen 2017).

Figure 21 includes several illustrations of common joining methods. Placing the edges of two pieces together is called an *edge joint*. In some cases, wood pieces may be glued together, but usually they are held together with additional pieces of wood. Often, complimentary holes or *mortises* are cut into the edges of two pieces of wood. Then a fitted, usually rectangular, piece of wood called a *tenon* can be inserted into the two mortises as all the pieces are brought together. This is called a *loose tenon and mortise system*. A hole could also be drilled through the two pieces, and a (usually) short, cylindrical piece of wood, called a *dowel*, can be inserted into them to hold the pieces in place. To create corners, the simplest way to join two pieces of wood is to place them together so that one abuts the other, which creates what is referred to as a *butt joint*. To more securely hold the pieces in place, a shoulder can be cut into one or both of the pieces. This is referred to as *half-lap* or *rebated butt joint*. Each edge of a piece of wood can be cut at a 45-degree angle, so that when connected they create a 90-degree angle. This is called a *mitre joint*. A *dovetail joint* involves cutting a dovetail shaped tongue or tail into one piece of wood, which is intended to fit into a corresponding socket in the other piece. Just like with the joining of an edge joint, a system of mortises and tenons or dowels can be used to hold these different joints in place. While these are the most common approaches, there are a variety of additional joint types, as well as other methods of holding the joints together.

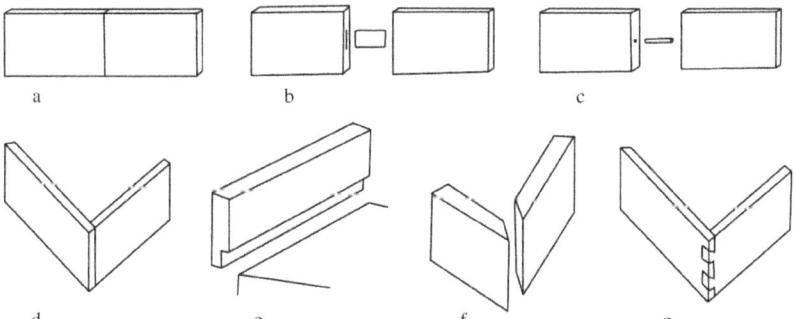

Figure 21 A selection of common woodworking joints. (a) edge joint, (b) edge joint connected with a loose mortise and tenon, (c) edge joint connected with a dowel, (d) butt joint, (e) half-lap joint/rebated butt joint, (f) mitre joint, (g) dovetail joint. Image by author.

6.3 Ethnoarchaeology and Assessing Ancient Woodworking

When attempting to interpret the static marks of woodworking, it is often helpful to observe modern communities in order to consider questions about how these static forms might be produced. This is an approach referred to as *ethnoarchaeology* (Politis 2020). Ethnoarchaeology is a form of analogy construction. As Alison Wylie (1985, 101) noted, archaeologists using analogies must always be careful that the modern and ancient factors being assessed can be reasonably connected; or as Richard Gould and Patty Watson (1982, 442) warned, scholars should avoid "a simple and direct reading of the past from the present." For woodworking, a possible use of ethnoarchaeology may mean watching modern woodworkers work with different tools, and then examining the tool marks that are produced. If similar tool marks can be found on the ancient material, it may be reasonable to suggest that similar tools were also used in both cases. Moreover, by witnessing the production of wooden objects, the archaeologist may gain insight into the various steps that the carpenter used to produce the object. The chain of operations used in production is often referred to in archaeological and anthropological literature as the *chaîne opératoire* (Lemonnier 1992, 26). This may inspire the archaeologist to look for additional evidence for such steps in the material record.

When using ethnoarchaeology, it is always important to consider how the modern analog may differ from the ancient process. Some elements are quite obvious – for instance, if the modern woodworkers are using electric tools, their work will be largely incompatible with this approach. Their system, time of work, materials, and the tool marks produced will be different than those found in preindustrial societies. Somewhat less obvious may be differences due to the material of the tools – steel tools, bronze tools, and stone tools, for instance, will involve different steps of production as well (Arbuckle 2018, 45). Moreover, when attempting to move beyond more technical or, as Wylie (1985, 94–95) calls them, "formal" comparisons between elements in order to gain a broader view of practice or society, even more care is required (Wendrich 2013, 192; Hodder 2013).

In my own work, for instance, I examined the practice of woodworkers in Cairo in order to assess the production of wooden objects in ancient Egypt (Arbuckle 2018, 27–44). These carpenters were working with tools that were similar to those used in ancient Egypt, and completing the types of joints and objects that were also fairly similar to those in the past. While this was helpful for interpreting the types of tool marks that their tools produced, I wanted to take my analysis further. All the individuals I spoke to also mentioned that it took four to five years of constant work alongside a master in order to confidently cut and shape wooden objects. They explained that by the end of this period, they had learnt how to hold tools properly, how to move their bodies to saw or strike the wood, and how to hold and hammer chisels. They now therefore worked smoothly through the woods and their tools rarely snagged. This type of physical competency is what Willeke Wendrich (2013, 12) refers to as "body knowledge." Speaking to other woodworkers in North America, these carpenters confirmed that this was the time it took them to learn as well. This then suggested that the work of carpenters who had trained for a significant space of time to be considered "skilled" might be visible through the tool marks they produced. While the initial ethnographic study had inspired this hypothesis, experimental archaeology was then used to test it (see Section 6.4).

6.4 Experimental Archaeology and Assessing Ancient Woodworking

Experimental Archaeology is another approach based on analogy. The scholar attempts to reproduce practices from the past themselves in order to gain a better understanding of the dynamic processes that produced the material record (Dvořáková 2024). As James Skibbo (1992, 18) put it, it allows archaeologists to replicate "materials, behaviors, or both, in order to observe one or more processes involved in the production, use, discard, deterioration, or recovery of material culture." In this case, the archaeologist would therefore attempt to create wooden objects themselves, using similar tools to those that would have been used in the ancient context. Depending on the questions being investigated, this may also include recreating tools, or selecting the timbers available to the community in question, to see how this may impact production and leave traces in the archaeological record. Eleni Maragoudaki (2019), for instance, recreated and tested replicas of Late Bronze Age saws from the Aegean to better understand the possible types of moulds that would have been used, the types of handles, how the shape of the saw would have impacted production, and more.

In my own work on ancient Egyptian woodworking, ethnographic analysis had suggested that tool marks may be able to demonstrate the work of skilled vs. unskilled carpenters – those who had been trained for four to five years to acquire the appropriate "body knowledge," and those who had not (see Section 6.3). In order to test this theory, I conducted an experiment with a group of carpenters in Los Angeles (Arbuckle 2018, 51–56). I acquired wood samples of the species of timber frequently used in ancient Egypt, as well as a modern pull-saw, similar to what would have been used in antiquity. I asked the professional woodworkers to saw through these different species of wood, after which I sawed through the same pieces. We were also timed while we worked. While I have some training in woodworking, I am not a professional, and have not had sufficient experience to gain the required "body knowledge" to move smoothly through wood with a pull saw – I often snag the wood and need to adjust my stance. I then compared our saw marks. The professional kerf marks were much more even and regular, while mine were much closer together, and changed direction more frequently as I adjusted my stance and hold. This helped to suggest what I should be looking for in the material record in order to assess whether work was done by an experienced carpenter or a beginner. This helped me to avoid more biased judgements about the quality of the finished product (see further Section 7). Of course, several other elements such as the hardness of the wood, access to different materials for tools, and more, need to be considered, but this has proven to be an excellent place to start.

6.5 Further Reading

For an accessible discussion of wood properties that impact construction, see Hoadley (2000). For a thorough discussion of Roman woodworking, which includes an overview of available tools, see Ulrich (2007). For a brief though detailed look at ancient Egyptian woodworking see Gale et al. (2000). For a thorough overview of Egyptian woodworking in different periods, see Killen (2017). For a brief introduction to modern carpentry and joinery, including a standard modern toolkit, see Bates (2013). For a brief introduction to ethnoarchaeology, Politis (2020) provides a good overview. For a brief introduction to experimental archaeology, see Dvořáková (2024).

7 Case Studies: Analyzing Wooden Coffins in Museums and in the Field

In this section, I discuss two case studies to show how the combination of scientific and humanistic methods can produce a more holistic understanding of archaeological wooden objects and the communities in which they were produced. These examples highlight two different projects: the analysis of an anthropoid 21st/22nd Dynasty (c. 1086–736 BCE) Egyptian coffin currently at the Denver Museum of Nature & Science; and the examination of one rectangular and one anthropoid 18th Dynasty (c. 1548–1302 BCE) coffin assessed in the field during excavations at Saqqara, Egypt. The practical realities of working in these very different spaces has a significant impact on the approach taken by the wood analyst, and shows how specialists must often adapt to their situations. Despite these compromises, however, the resulting analyses can nevertheless provide significant insights into the human past, helping to demonstrate the importance of including wood experts in both contexts.

7.1 Coffin EX1997-24.4 at the Denver Museum of Nature & Science

In 2016, an interdisciplinary group of scholars gathered at the Denver Museum of Nature & Science to conduct a series of analyses on two mummies and three coffins (Koons and Arbuckle MacLeod 2021a). These analyses included scanning the objects and human remains using computed tomography (CT scans) (Hayes et al. 2021), an Egyptological/art historical examination of the coffin decoration (Howley et al. 2021), and material analyses of the pigments using gas chromatography-mass spectrometry (Price et al. 2021). A series of analyses were also directed specifically at understanding the wood and construction of the coffins, which are, of course, the aspects of most interest presently. Here I limit myself to a discussion of the analysis of only one coffin, anonymous coffin EX1997-24.4 (see Figure 22). The coffin had come to Colorado in 1905 in the possession of a private collector, Andrew McClelland, though it is believed to have originally come from Thebes, Egypt (Koons and Arbuckle MacLeod 2021b, 14).

7.1.1 Wood Analysis of Coffin EX1997-24.4

To begin the wood analysis of EX1997-24.4, samples were taken from the coffin at the Denver Museum of Nature & Science. The coffins were laid out on tables by the museum staff, and then these objects were examined to locate the best areas for sampling. The coffins were all plastered, painted, and covered over with a varnish, and the lid of coffin EX1997-24.4 could not be turned over, so samples had to be taken from the exterior. Ideally, every piece of wood used to construct a coffin would be sampled. Egyptologists are well aware that pieces of wood from multiple species of trees could be combined in a single coffin (Dawson and Strudwick 2016, 184–89; Cartwright 2019). This is especially true for the historical period to which this coffin dated, the 21st or 22nd Dynasty (c. 1086–736 BCE) within Egypt's Third Intermediate Period. This is a time when the reuse of wood was more common than in previous eras (Cooney 2011).

It is rarely possible, however, to take the ideal number of samples, particularly for decorated coffins, and particularly in museum settings. Here, the objects have already been cleaned and have usually gone through an extensive conservation process; moreover, the priority of the museum curators must be to preserve the integrity of the object. Nevertheless, working closely with the curators, we found broken areas at the shoulders of the coffin where the wood was exposed, far enough away from additional decoration that the risk of the wood cells being infused with pigments or varnishes was minimal. Altogether four samples were taken from the lid: one from the right shoulder, one from the

Figure 22 Lid of Coffin EX1997-24.4. Image used with permission from the Denver Museum of Nature & Science.

left shoulder, and two from the joining elements, one tenon and one dowel. While the case of the coffin was largely avoided due to extensive decoration, a sample from a final dowel was taken from here as well (see Section 6.2.3; Arbuckle MacLeod et al. 2021, 98–100). The samples were taken by hand with a scalpel and tweezers, and were approximately 2.5 mm^3.

Some of the samples were then examined in a laboratory at the campus of the University of California, Los Angeles. The procedure for analysis followed that laid out in Section 4.2. Thin sections for each plane of reference were prepared, and these were initially examined using transmitted light microscopy. To examine additional details on the wood specimens, several were selected for SEM. For this analysis, the samples were fractured to expose the three planes of reference and mounted on carbon tape on stubs. They were examined using a variable pressure FEI NOVA 230 Nano SEM at Low Vacuum (LV) with a Low Vacuum Detector (LVD) (Arbuckle MacLeod et al. 2021, 97–98). The anatomical features were then compared with reference specimens. The results of this analysis demonstrated that the two samples from the sides of the coffin, the main coffin planks, were *Ficus sycomorus*, sycomore fig, while the two dowels and tenons were *Vachellia nilotica*, acacia. Both of these species are local hardwoods found in Egypt (Arbuckle MacLeod et al. 2021, 98–100).

Three of the samples, one from the main coffin wood of the lid, the tenon from the lid, and the dowel from the case, were also sent off for radiocarbon dating. The radiocarbon dates for the tenon and dowel were very similar, and supplied a range of 909 to 837 calBCE. The radiocarbon date for the lid, however, was 1016–936 calBCE (Koons and Arbuckle MacLeod 2021b, 25). From the artistic and textual analysis, the final decoration of the coffin likely took place towards the end of the Egyptian 21st Dynasty (c. 970 BCE), or the first half of the 22nd Dynasty (c. 870 BCE). The acacia radiocarbon dates are more firmly within the 22nd Dynasty, while the sycomore fig dates straddle the two periods.

The wood analysis and dates may suggest that the sycomore fig was older than the acacia. As sycomore fig is a slow-growing tree, it is possible that this is a case of the "old wood problem" (see Section 5.4); however, CT scans of the coffin wood suggest that the areas where the samples were taken were from the outermost tree-rings – particularly suggestive is the presence of bark in some areas (see Section 7.1.2), and so it is unlikely that the samples differed in date by a century to the true felling date of the tree. It is more likely that the sycomore fig wood was reused from an older object or architectural feature, as so commonly occurred in the Third Intermediate Period in Egypt. The close association between the dates of the acacia and the art historical analysis suggest that the acacia timbers were cut shortly before the coffin was to be constructed (Arbuckle MacLeod et al. 2021, 106).

7.1.2 The Construction of Coffin EX1997-24.4

It is usually difficult to comment on the construction of wooden anthropoid coffins from ancient Egypt. These objects are frequently covered with layers of plaster/paste, paint, and resinous varnishes, which often cover up joints and tool marks. For this example, however, some areas of the decoration had fallen off, and CT scans of the coffins were completed, providing excellent insights into the internal construction (see Figure 23). The scans showed that the initial conversion method for some planks of the wood was the through-and-through method, accomplished with saws, creating plainsawn boards. For other areas of the construction, however, roundwood timbers were used with little initial reduction, as the bark was still present on some pieces. The roughly shaped boards of the coffin were largely edge or butt joined together with long dowels, though a few areas indicated more complicated joints: a stub tenon and mortise joint and a wedge joint were used to attach areas of the sides of the coffin, and a half-dovetail joint was used to attach the footboard to the lid. Loose mortise and tenon joints were only used to join the central planks of the lid and to lock this lid in place on the case (Arbuckle MacLeod 2021, 78–79). There were also significant gaps left between the joints, and these were simply filled with thick layers of plaster.

As noted in the previous section (7.1.1), the main wood used for the larger planks of the coffin was identified as sycomore fig, while the dowels and tenon were acacia. These are both local hardwood species available throughout ancient and modern Egypt. Sycomore fig is the timber most frequently selected for coffin construction, but it is a fairly light weight timber. Carpenters generally refer to the *specific gravity* of wood when discussing its density and strength. This is defined as "the decimal ratio of the oven-dry weight of a piece of wood to the weight of the water displaced by the wood at a given moisture content" (Newsom 2022, 7). Generally speaking, the higher the specific gravity, the denser the wood. Sycomore fig has a specific gravity of 0.48 (CABI 2022).

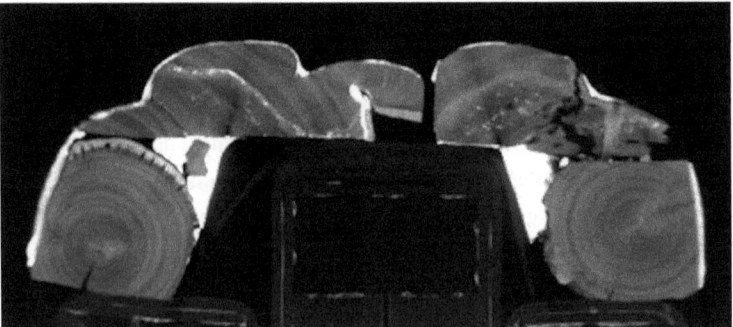

Figure 23 A CT scan of coffin EX1997-24.4, showing the use of roundwood on the sides. The bright white portions demonstrate the use of plaster fills. Used with permission from the Denver Museum of Nature & Science.

Acacia nilotica on the other hand, has a specific gravity of 0.67–0.68 (Dorostkar 2015, 749). It seems then, that the carpenters selected a stronger wood which would be better suited for the dowels and tenons. These pieces would be put under greater stress while holding the coffin wood together. This is a fairly common practice for ancient Egyptian carpenters (Cartwright 2016), as demonstrated through this example and those noted further (Sections 7.2.1 and 7.2.2).

Where the decorative layers had fallen off the coffin, tool marks were visible. This demonstrates that the carpenters had not undertaken the final steps of smoothing the coffin before applying the base plaster layer. This is generally associated with a faster and lower-quality approach to construction, as the plaster and paint are more likely to fall off rough surfaces, as was indeed the case in many areas on this coffin. On the exposed footboard, kerf marks were left that show even, and largely parallel saw strokes, down the face of the wood (Arbuckle MacLeod 2021, 80). On the body of the coffin, uniform, slightly scooped facets are visible, demonstrating the skilled use of an adze to shape the anthropoid form. Together, these regular, even marks suggest the work of an experienced carpenter, who had acquired the "body knowledge" necessary to competently move with his tools (Wendrich 2012, 13; Arbuckle MacLeod 2021, 81–82).

The selection of the wood, and the evidence for "body knowledge," speaks to the work of experienced carpenters; however, a number of additional details suggest that the carpenters were working quickly, and not particularly carefully. These include the fact that bark was left on the wood in some areas; extensive amounts of plaster were used to fill gaps, instead of ensuring better fitting joints; and that the tool marks were not smoothed away. This would produce a finished product that would look high-quality thanks to the finished addition of the plaster, paint, and varnishes, but may not last as long as other examples of coffins. These additional added materials may also suggest information about the coffin's owner. Egyptian blue pigment and imported varnishes were used in its decoration and perhaps for final burial rituals. These were expensive materials and speak to the overall higher cost of the coffin, and the possibly related higher status of its owner (Arbuckle MacLeod 2021, 85). This all suggests that the frequent reuse of timber and coffins from this period may have encouraged the Egyptians to focus on the initial ritual function of the coffin during the burial. They may have therefore invested their means in the visible decoration, while demonstrating less concern with the long-term preservation of the full coffin. This differs from apparent construction priorities in earlier periods of Egypt's history (Arbuckle MacLeod and Cooney 2019; Arbuckle MacLeod 2021, 89–90; for more on coffin reuse, see Cooney 2024). Parts of the wood for this coffin may indeed have been reused, and the coffin itself was also reused, as it ultimately contained the mummy of an individual who died 600 years after the construction dates.

7.2 The Saqqara Coffins

In 2023, I joined the Leiden-Turin Archaeological Expedition to Saqqara, Egypt. This was led by a team from the Museo Egizio in Turin, and the National Museum of Antiquities (RMO) in Leiden (a full preliminary report for this season of the project is in production: Del Vesco forthcoming). I had a number of goals as the wood specialist, among them a re-analysis of two coffins that had been discovered in 1999, during a previous excavation of the site (van Walsem et al. 1999; Raven et al. 2011). The coffins had been found in separate pit burials just to the south of the commander Horemheb's tomb, very close to the exterior wall of his inner courtyard (van Walsem et al. 1999, 19, 23–24). The coffins were published in both a preliminary report and in a more detailed publication that consolidated the data of several years of work. These publications consisted of expert discussions, including those by the excavators and previous material specialists. The initial publications provided a thorough discussion of the context of the coffins, their preservation state, and an overview of the decoration and translations of the remaining hieroglyphic inscriptions on both coffins. The authors had also provided line drawings and an overview of basic construction details (Raven et al. 2011, 76–81). Based on a combination of the find context, associated pottery, and decorative elements, the date proposed for both coffins was the 18th Dynasty, probably around the reign of Amenhotep III (c. 1389–1349 BCE) or slightly later (van Walsem et al. 1999, 23). Since their initial discovery, the coffins had been kept in a secure storage area at Saqqara. While the initial discussion was quite thorough, no wood analysis was completed, and the recent excavators believed that this, and an additional examination of the construction, might reveal significant information. The designations for the coffins provided by the initial excavators, Coffin 127A and 130A, are maintained in the present discussion.

Before beginning analysis, I set up a microscopy station on the site (Figure 24). This was located within the tomb of Horemheb, in the inner courtyard, in an area that was largely protected from the wind and had access to electricity. All samples had to be assessed on site, as it is generally not permitted to remove samples from Egypt and access to local analysis equipment is limited. For this analysis, I used a Swift SW380T Compound Microscope for transmitted light microscopy. This is a light-weight, portable microscope that is inexpensive but has camera attachments for photography, and allows clear imagery of features up to around 800x magnification.

Figure 24 A mobile wood analysis station on site in the field at Saqqara, Egypt. Image by author.

7.2.1 Analysis of Coffin 127A (Hesynebef)

Coffin 127A belonged to an individual referred to as Hesynebef in its somewhat garbled inscriptions. It is a rectangular coffin with a gabled lid, and a black painted background, decorated with yellow figures and texts that were fairly typical for the period (Figure 25). The original excavators noted that the preservation of the coffin was poor – it had been found in a fairly fragmentary state, and the base of the coffin no longer survived. To begin my analysis, I laid out the surviving fragments, and found evidence of additional deterioration. The majority of the damage seems to have been done by ancient and modern insects and arachnids. Several spiders' nests were visible through the fragments, and significant termite and beetle damage was clear from extensive tunnelling. Several fragments of the coffin, which appeared initially intact, had been rendered almost entirely frass, the remnants of insect damage (see Section 3.2.3). They were largely held together by the thick amounts of plaster and paint that had covered the coffin. Despite these drawbacks, the remaining pieces included large planks that retained complete joints, held together by a combination of tenons and dowels that were able to provide significant timber and construction data.

Figure 25 Side of Coffin 127A belonging to a Hesynebef. Image by author.

To begin, I measured and assessed each of the fragments separately to determine which ones had enough surviving wood material to permit an anatomical assessment. Of the 66 remaining coffin fragments, many were very small, others were just frass, or in some cases just plaster. A few were also made up of wads of plastered linen that had clearly been stuffed into gaps in the construction and plastered and painted over in order to allow the coffin to appear whole. Ultimately, 36 pieces were wooden fragments, only one of which was too deteriorated to permit analysis. For the remaining 35 fragments, small samples of approximately 2 mm^3 were taken from areas that were least affected by the additional materials or insect damage. Thin sections from the three planes of reference were then created for each sample, and examined with the microscope. The features were then compared with reference images from the InsideWood online database and a personal collection of physical vouchered samples of modern specimens.

Of the 35 identifiable fragments, 30 pieces were from the main planks of the coffin, one was a tenon, and four were dowels. The 30 plank fragments were identified as *Ficus sycomorus*, sycomore fig. The tenon and two dowels were *Vachellia nilotica* (acacia), and the remaining two dowels were *Tamarix* spp. (tamarisk), all local Egyptian hardwoods. As with the coffin discussed previously (Section 7.1.2), it is likely that the carpenters chose to use harder woods for the connecting elements of the coffin. Like acacia, tamarisk has a higher specific gravity than sycomore fig, of around 0.60–0.73 (Mantanis and Birbilis 2010, 86), and so is also an appropriate choice for this context.

Turning now to the construction details, the planks for the coffins were plainsawn. These were then edge-joined with loose mortise and tenon joints, held in place with additional dowels. At the corners, the coffin was connected with dovetail joints. Kerf marks and facets from saws and chisels were visible in a number of areas where the paint had fallen away, suggesting that little effort was spent on smoothing or finishing the wood surface. In addition, there were a number of gaps and faults in pieces that were either filled with thick amounts of plaster or, as noted earlier, filled with wads of linen. Another interesting feature, and one that had not been mentioned in the previous publications, was that many of the interior joints of the coffin had been painted red.

The general craftsmanship, the use of more complicated joining techniques, and regular kerf marks, suggest that this coffin was created by experienced carpenters. As they had not removed the tool marks, however, and had simply filled large gaps with plaster or textiles, it was clear that the overall quality of the construction was poor. A number of corners were cut to avoid either finding better quality wood, or creating better fitting patches and joints. A lack of expensive materials used in the coffin construction, along with a lack of prestigious additional burial implements, would suggest that the owner was not particularly high ranking; nevertheless, they clearly did have enough disposable wealth to afford a coffin, and so the owner was probably of a lower ranking elite (for a discussion of coffin expenses and status, see Arbuckle MacLeod 2021, 85).

The use of the dovetail joints on this coffin is particularly interesting. From the end of the Old Kingdom, through to the end of the Middle Kingdom in ancient Egypt, a period of about 600 years, the vast majority of rectangular coffins had been created with almost the same construction method: long rectangular coffins with the edges joined through the use of a mitre joint surmounted by a butt joint. At the end of the Middle Kingdom, however, the use of dovetail joint corners begins to take over, and by the 18th Dynasty, virtually all recovered rectangular coffins are joined with dovetail joints (Arbuckle MacLeod 2023b). The majority of our evidence for this transition, however, comes from Upper Egypt (the southern area), particularly the site of Thebes. This northern piece from Saqqara therefore adds a significant example to our understanding of craftsmanship, and suggests that this trend was indeed Egypt-wide. This further adds to our understanding that coffin carpenters were likely in communication, perhaps joined in networks of crafting communities.

To add to this interpretation is the presence of the red paint on the joints. The widespread nature of this tradition is quickly becoming appreciated by the Egyptological community (Arbuckle 2018: 210–211; Arbuckle MacLeod and Cooney 2019, n.46; Eschenbrenner Diemer et al. 2021; Arbuckle MacLeod 2023a). Red was frequently used to protect thresholds in ancient Egypt, and so this seems to be an effort made by the carpenters to protect the vulnerable spaces of the coffin from the possible intrusion of evil forces after the burial. Our evidence for this practice from the mid-late second millennium BCE, Egypt's so-called New Kingdom, is again more robust for southern Egypt, so this example helps to add to the full repertoire. It also demonstrates that these carpenters had religious knowledge, knowledge that seems to have been passed

70   *Current Archaeological Tools and Techniques*

between communities for generations. This tradition also seems to continue despite other changes to construction – such as the shift to dovetail joints.

7.2.2 Analysis of Coffin 130A (Anonymous)

The anthropoid (human-shaped) coffin 130A was also found in a poor state of preservation. Only parts of the lid survived, and those were again significantly damaged by insects (see Figure 26). The decoration of the coffin consisted of a black painted background, making up the body of the lid, with polychrome decoration applied on top. A fragmentary image of the goddess Nut stretched

Figure 26 Remains of anthropoid coffin 130A. Image by author.

across the lower half of the lid, with a very damaged inscription written down the centre. The top third of the lid consisted of a white face with black painted details and a black-and-white striped wig. Hands, carved as fists, were added to the front, crossing the chest. A floral collar and bracelets or arm bands were represented through stripes of blue, red, and white paint (Raven et al. 2011, 81). The method of analysis for wood and construction was the same as the previous coffin (see Section 7.2.1).

Of the 59 remaining coffin fragments, 21 were wooden pieces large and stable enough to permit analysis. 17 of these fragments were major elements of the coffin, and included the planks, the carved hands, wig, and footboard (the face was not available for analysis in the 2023 season). Four pieces were dowels. All of the 17 major elements were identified as *Ficus sycomorus* (sycomore fig), while all four dowels were *Tamarix* spp. (a species of tamarisk). For the selection of woods, this once again demonstrates the previously discussed priorities of Egyptian carpenters who tended to use sycomore fig for the larger pieces, and harder species for the connective elements (see Sections 7.1.1 and 7.2.1).

The construction of the coffin consisted largely of long, edge-joined planks, with separately carved wig lappets and hands. All of these pieces were held together with dowels. A large carved block of wood was then added as the footboard of the coffin, connected with a large dovetail joint (see Figure 27). The planks of the coffin were plainsawn, preserving the most wood possible. The only mortise and loose tenon joints that remained were used at the edges of

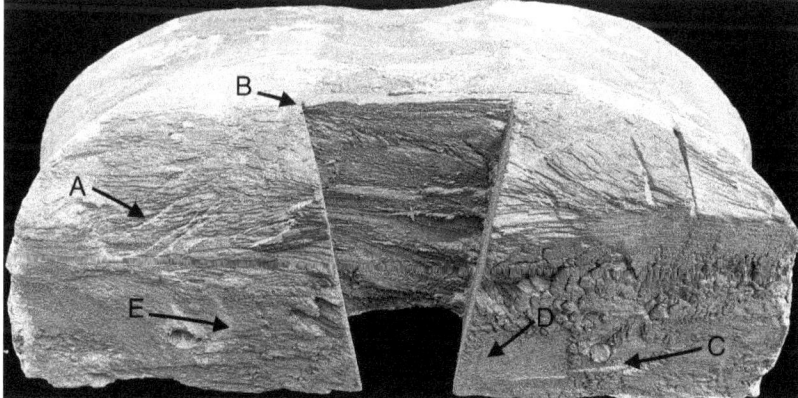

Figure 27 The interior of the foot block from coffin 130A, showing construction details and tool marks. (A) Saw kerf marks, (B) kerf, (C) chisel facet, (D) red cutting guideline, (E) remnants of red paint for religious/protective purposes.

the lid, supposedly to hold the lid on to the case. There were rough tool marks visible in the areas not covered with plaster or paint, showing the kerf marks of saws and facets of chisel marks. While plaster was added to fill out gaps, no wads of linen were included. As with the previous coffin, many of the coffin joints demonstrated the presence of red paint, again suggesting the work of carpenters with religious and perhaps ritual knowledge (see Section 7.2.1, Figure 14, E).

While most of the construction is fairly standard for New Kingdom anthropoid coffins, the tool marks on the footboard provide some additional insights into the actions and choices of ancient Egyptian carpenters (see Figure 14). Even saw marks are clear down the face of the foot block. A saw was also clearly used to carve the large dovetail socket, with a kerf extending slightly too far into the block. Some additional facets on the face and the joint show the subsequent use of a chisel for additional shaping. A final interesting detail is the presence of a thin red line, about 1 cm from the cut for the dovetail socket. This is clearly a construction guideline drawn by the carpenter, who decided at the last moment to cut slightly to the inside of their line. This therefore suggests an ancient instance of the old carpentry adage, "measure twice, cut once." All together these construction details show experienced carpenters who are working quite quickly, but nevertheless provided a fairly well-constructed anthropoid coffin for their clientele.

In this case, the anthropoid coffin is a bit puzzling. A number of prestigious objects were found associated with the burial (Raven et al. 2011, 81). The coffin itself, however, does not include costly varnishes, nor is the construction particularly careful, as seen with other elite coffins from this period. Perhaps the owner died unexpectedly and a quickly constructed coffin was necessary for the burial, or they decided to invest their wealth in other elements of the burial assemblage.

7.3 Assessing Archaeological Wood in Museums versus the Field

In both of these case studies, the wood and construction analysis of coffins added to our understanding of crafting choices in ancient Egypt within different periods. The approach to analysis differed in significant ways, however, based on whether the work was carried out in a museum or in the field. In the museum, the objects are usually very high-quality, decorated pieces, that would be attractive to visitors. They have also usually been thoroughly cleaned and conserved. This means that curators are much more hesitant to allow sampling, particularly multiple samples from different areas of the coffin. The curators from the Denver Museum of Nature & Science, however, were particularly dedicated to conducting multiple elements of analysis on their collection; they wanted to better understand the histories of these objects and the people represented by the human remains they contained. This was otherwise a challenge due to a lack of a definitive find context. They therefore understood that small samples, which would not greatly impact the aesthetic integrity of the object, would be valuable. Due to the conserved state of the coffin, and areas that were covered with paint and resins, only a limited number of samples could be taken. The museum also had more access to specialists, including medical personnel who could conduct CT scans on the coffins, which greatly improved the ability to examine construction details. Finally, the samples could be taken back to a formal laboratory for analysis, enabling the use of SEM.

In the field, the coffins that I analyzed were not well preserved. Due to their preservation state, they were not deemed museum quality, and so were not taken for display. While this meant that in some areas the wood was in too severe a state of decay to analyze, enough samples could be taken from enough of the coffin elements to be confident about providing a representative analysis of how different timber species were combined for construction. While this allowed more flexibility for the approach to assessment, the fact that all the analysis equipment had to be brought to site meant that only light weight and relatively low-power instruments could be used. The number of additional specialists who could provide insights are also comparatively limited, as each specialist needs to be transported to site, and only those analyses that can be done on site can be carried out. Nevertheless, the excellent contextual information for the coffins found on excavation ensures that the background information for the objects is more readily accessible.

In both cases, the work of multiple experts, whether this be the efforts of previous excavators and epigraphers in Saqqara, or the multi-disciplinary group in Denver, contributed significant information to assist with the interpretation of the coffin construction. The wood analysis provided insights into ancient Egyptian society and the skills, knowledge, and beliefs of ancient carpenters. This helps to show how material analyses such as wood analysis are able to provide a more holistic view of ancient objects and communities that goes well beyond the object owner.

7.4 Further Readings

For the complete discussion of the analyses performed on the coffins and mummies from the Denver Museum of Nature & Science, see Koons and Arbuckle MacLeod (2021a). For more information about the excavations and coffins at Saqqara, see van Walsem et al. (1999) and Raven et al. (2011).

8 Final Thoughts

In the preceding sections I have discussed a number of elements of archaeological wood analysis. This includes significant and diverse studies from the hard sciences, including an introduction to tree growth and the chemistry of wood, common biological factors impacting wood preservation, and a basic overview of wood anatomy and tree-ring sciences. All archaeologists who may come into contact with wooden objects and remnants, which includes all excavators, should have this basic understanding of wood material. This will ensure that they are equipped to make choices between different sampling options, and to understand what is necessary for anatomical and dendrochronological analyses. This knowledge is even imperative for interpreting carbon 14 dates, which are so commonly conducted on wood remnants. Nevertheless, wood science seems to remain a rather rare element of general archaeological studies. This has caused significant lacks in data and problematic analyses. I often receive emails from archaeologists with blurry photos of large wooden objects asking, "what wood is this?" Hopefully it is now clear to those reading this Element why wood analysis cannot be done in this manner. On the other hand, scientific publications of archaeological wood analysis are too often written in overly technical language. This makes them impenetrable for non-specialists. So some confusion regarding the process is understandable. The present work has therefore attempted to provide an accessible bridge between these two communities, and to demonstrate just how much potential information can be obtained from archaeological wooden remains.

This potential information is also not limited to biological or chemical analyses. Wooden objects, as with so many other types of archaeological evidence, can also be used to answer social questions about the human past. These aspects enter too infrequently into more technical discussions. Tool marks and the steps of production can reveal the choices and training of carpenters, the organization of their work, and the values of their patrons, elements of society that are too often ignored in written histories. When these investigations are combined with the additional scientific analyses, holistic interpretations can provide insights into a much broader picture of everyday life in the past. This is particularly important for areas that have superior preservation of wooden objects. If we are able to highlight the ubiquity, function, and significance of wooden materials in these communities, we will also better understand the massive lacuna in our evidence from other regions. Wood is and has always been one of the fundamental construction materials used by humans living at all times and in almost all areas of the world. The question is therefore almost never *was* wood used here, but *how*. As more wood specialists are trained and involved in archaeological analyses, hopefully we will begin to have a better understanding of the history of this valuable and ubiquitous material.

References

Altobelli, Annarita, Paola Cennamo, Giorgio Trojsi, et al. 2023. "Experimentation of a PVA-Borax Hydrogel for the Removal of Paraloid B72® from Artifacts of Archaeological Interest from the National Archaeological Museum in Naples, Italy." *Acta IMEKO* 12 (3): 1–8. https://doi.org/10.21014/actai meko.v12i3.1501.

Amusant. 2023. "Wood Extractives: Main Families, Functional Properties, Fields of Application and Interest of Wood Waste." *Forest Products Journal* 73 (3): 194–208.

Arbuckle, Caroline. 2018. "A Social History of Coffins and Carpenters." PhD Dissertation. Los Angeles: University of California, Los Angeles. https://escholarship.org/uc/item/1b81337z.

Arbuckle MacLeod, Caroline. 2021. "The Creation of a Third Intermediate Period Coffin: Coffin EX1997-24.4 in the Denver Museum of Nature & Science." In *The Egyptian Mummies and Coffins of the Denver Museum of Nature & Science: History, Technical Analysis, and Conservation*, edited by Michele L. Koons and Caroline Arbuckle MacLeod, 72–92. Louisville: University Press of Colorado.

——— 2023a. "The Social Pyramid and the Status of Craftspeople in Ancient Egypt." In *Ancient Egyptian Society: Challenging Assumptions, Exploring Approaches*, edited by Danielle Candelora, Nadia Ben-Marzouk, and Kara Cooney, 62–73. New York: Routledge.

——— 2023b. "The Significance of Coffin Construction Practices in the Old and Middle Kingdoms." *Claroscuro* 22 (2): 1–35. https://doi.org/10.35305/cl.vi22.136.

——— 2024. "Lebanese Cedar, Skeuomorphs, Coffins, and Status in Ancient Egypt." *Arts* 13 (6): 163. https://doi.org/10.3390/arts13060163.

Arbuckle MacLeod, Caroline, and Kathlyn M. Cooney. 2019. "The Layered Life of JE26204: The Construction and Reuse of the Coffins of Henuttawy." *The Journal of Egyptian Archaeology* 105 (2): 285–96. https://doi.org/10.1177/0307513320911383.

Arbuckle MacLeod, Caroline, Pearce Paul Creasman, and Christopher H. Baisan. 2021. "Coffin Timbers and Dendrochronology: The Significance of Wood in Coffins from the Denver Museum of Nature & Science." In *The Egyptian Mummies and Coffins of the Denver Museum of Nature & Science: History, Technical Analysis, and Conservation*, edited by Michele L. Koons and Caroline Arbuckle MacLeod, 93–110. Louisville: University Press of Colorado.

Arzola-Villegas, Xavier, Carlos Báez, Roderic Lakes, et al. 2023. "Convolutional Neural Network for Segmenting Micro-X-Ray Computed Tomography Images of Wood Cellular Structures." *Applied Sciences* 13 (14): 8146. https://doi.org/10.3390/app13148146.

Asouti, Eleni, and Phil Austin. 2005. "Reconstructing Woodland Vegetation and Its Exploitation by Past Societies, Based on the Analysis and Interpretation of Archaeological Wood Charcoal Macro-Remains." *Environmental Archaeology* 10 (1): 1–18. https://doi.org/10.1179/env.2005.10.1.1.

Baillie, Michael G. L. 1995. *A Slice through Time: Dendrochronology and Precision Dating*. London: Batsford.

Barham, Lawrence, Geoffrey A. T. Duller, Ian Candy, et al. 2023. "Evidence for the Earliest Structural Use of Wood at Least 476,000 Years Ago." *Nature* 622 (7981): 107–11. https://doi.org/10.1038/s41586-023-06557-9.

Bates, David R. 2013. *Carpentry and Joinery*. Second. Oxon [England]: Routledge.

Beattie, Owen, Brian Apland, Erik W. Blake, et al. 2000. "The Kwädāy Dän Ts'ínchi Discovery from a Glacier in British Columbia." *Canadian Journal of Archaeology / Journal Canadien d'Archéologie* 24 (1): 129–47.

Bill, Jan, Aoife Daly, Øistein Johnsen, and Knut S. Dalen. 2012. "DendroCT – Dendrochronology without Damage." *Dendrochronologia* 30 (3): 223–30. https://doi.org/10.1016/j.dendro.2011.11.002.

Blanchette, Robert A. 1998. "A Guide to Wood Deterioration Caused by Microorganisms and Insects." In *The Structural Conservation of Panel Paintings: Proceedings of a Symposium at the J. Paul Getty Museum, 24–28 April 1995*, edited by Kathleen Dardes, Andrea Rothe, J. Paul Getty Museum, and Getty Conservation Institute, 55–68. Los Angeles: Getty Conservation Institute.

Blanchette, Robert A., Benjamin W. Held, Joel A. Jurgens, et al. 2004. "Wood-Destroying Soft Rot Fungi in the Historic Expedition Huts of Antarctica." *Applied and Environmental Microbiology* 70 (3): 1328–35. https://doi.org/10.1128/AEM.70.3.1328-1335.2004.

Blanchette, Robert A., Thomas Nilsson, Geoffrey Daniel, and André Abad. 1990. "Biological Degradation of Wood." In *Archaeological Wood*, edited by Roger M. Rowell and R. James Barbour, 141–74. Washington, D.C.: American Chemical Society. Advances in Chemistry 225. American Chemical Society. https://doi.org/10.1021/ba-1990-0225.ch006.

Blondel, François, Manon Cabanis, Olivier Girardclos, and Sandrine Grenouillet-Paradis. 2018. "Impact of Carbonization on Growth Rings: Dating by

Dendrochronology Experiments on Oak Charcoals Collected from Archaeological Sites." *Quaternary International*, Anthracology: Local to Global Significance of Charcoal Science – Part III, 463 (January): 268–81. https://doi.org/10.1016/j.quaint.2017.03.030.

Brady, Timothy J. 1989. "The Influence of Flotation on the Rate of Recovery of Wood Charcoal from Archaeological Sites." *Journal of Ethnobiology* 9 (2): 207–27.

Broda, Magdalena, and Callum A. S. Hill, eds. 2022. *Historical Wood: Structure, Properties and Conservation*. Basel: MDPI.

Bronk Ramsey, Christopher, Hans van der Plicht, and Bernhard Weninger. 2001. "'Wiggle Matching' Radiocarbon Dates." *Radiocarbon* 43 (January): 381–89. https://doi.org/10.1017/S0033822200038248.

Brunning, Richard, and Jacqui Watson. 2010. *Waterlogged Wood: Guidelines on the Recording, Sampling, Conservation and Curation of Waterlogged Wood*. Swindon: English Heritage.

CABI. 2022. "Ficus Sycomorus (Sycamore Fig)." https://doi.org/10.1079/cabicompendium.24184.

Cartwright, Caroline R. 2016. "Wood in Ancient Egypt: Choosing Wood for Coffins." In *Death on the Nile: Uncovering the Afterlife of Ancient Egypt*, edited by Julie Dawson and Helen M Strudwick, 78–79. Cambridge (GB): The Fitzwilliam Museum.

2019. "Identifying Ancient Egyptian Coffin Woods from the Fitzwilliam Museum, Cambridge Using Scanning Electron Microscopy." In *Ancient Egyptian Coffins: Past – Present – Future*, edited by Helen Strudwick and Julie Dawson, 1–12. Oxford: Oxbow Books. https://doi.org/10.2307/j.ctvh9w0cw.

2020. "Understanding Wood Choices for Ancient Panel Painting and Mummy Portraits in the APPEAR Project through Scanning Electron Microscopy." In *Mummy Portraits of Roman Egypt: Emerging Research from the APPEAR Project*, edited by Marie Svoboda and Caroline Cartwright, 1st ed., 16–23. Los Angeles: J. Paul Getty Museum.

Cartwright, Caroline R., Lin Rosa Spaabæk, and Marie Svoboda. 2011. "Portrait Mummies from Roman Egypt: Ongoing Collaborative Research on Wood Identification." *British Museum Technical Research Bulletin* 5: 49–58.

Chabal, Lucie, Laurent Fabre, Jean-Frédéric Terral, and Isabelle Théry-Parisot. 1999. "L'Anthracologie." In *La Botanique*, edited by Christine Bourquin-Mignot, Jacques-Elie Brochier, Lucie Chabal, et al., 43–104. Archéologiques. Paris: Errance.

Coles, John M. ed. 1975–1989. *Somerset Levels Papers*. Somerset: Somerset Levels Project. https://doi.org/10.5284/1097701.

Cook, Robert A., and Aaron R. Comstock. 2014. "Evaluating the Old Wood Problem in a Temperate Climate: A Fort Ancient Case Study." *American Antiquity* 79 (4): 763–75.

Cooney, Kara. 2024. *Recycling for Death: Coffin Reuse in Ancient Egypt and the Theban Royal Caches*. Cairo: AUC Press.

Cooney, Kathlyn M. 2011. "Changing Burial Practices at the End of the New Kingdom: Defensive Adaptations in Tomb Commissions, Coffin Commissions, Coffin Decoration, and Mummification." *Journal of the American Research Center in Egypt* 47: 3–44. https://doi.org/10.2307/24555384.

Crivellaro, Alan, Fritz H. Schweingruber, and Charalambos S. Christodoulou. 2013. *Atlas of Wood, Bark and Pith Anatomy of Eastern Mediterranean Trees and Shrubs: With a Special Focus on Cyprus*. Berlin Heidelberg: Springer. https://doi.org/10.1007/978-3-642-37235-3.

D'Alpoim Guedes, Jade, and Robert Spengler. 2014. "Sampling Strategies in Paleoethnobotanical Analysis." In *Method and Theory in Paleoethnobotany*, edited by John M. Marston, Jade D'Alpoim Guedes, and Christina Warinner, 77–94. Boulder: University Press of Colorado. https://doi.org/10.5876/9781607323167.c005.

Dawson, Julie, and Helen M. Strudwick. 2016. *Death on the Nile: Uncovering the Afterlife of Ancient Egypt*. Cambridge: The Fitzwilliam Museum.

De Geus, André R., Sérgio F. Da Silva, Alexandre B. Gontijo, et al. 2020. "An Analysis of Timber Sections and Deep Learning for Wood Species Classification." *Multimedia Tools and Applications* 79 (45–46): 34513–29. https://doi.org/10.1007/s11042-020-09212-x.

Del Vesco, Paolo, Christian Greco, Daniel Soliman, Nico Staring, and Lara Weiss. Forthcoming. "The Leiden-Turin Archaeological Expedition to Saqqara: Preliminary Results of the 2022 and 2023 Fieldwork Seasons." *Rivista del Museo Egizio*.

Dierickx, Sofie, Siska Genbrugge, Hans Beeckman, et al. 2024. "Non-Destructive Wood Identification Using X-Ray CT Scanning: Which Resolution Do We Need?" *Plant Methods* 20: 98. https://doi.org/10.1186/s13007-024-01216-0

Dorostkar, Alireza. 2015. "Investigating the Properties of 'Acacia Nilotica' as a Species with Capability of Utilization in Furniture Industry." *International Journal of Innovative Science, Engineering & Technology* 1 (10): 748–52.

Douglass, Andrew E. 1920. "Evidence of Climatic Effects in the Annual Rings of Trees." *Ecology* 1 (1): 24–32. https://doi.org/10.2307/1929253.

———. 1935. *Dating Pueblo Bonito and Other Ruins of the Southwest*. 1. Washington, DC: National Geographic Society.

———. 1941. "Crossdating in Dendrochronology." *Journal of Forestry* 39: 825–31.

Dussol, Lydie, Michelle Elliott, Grégory Pereira, and Dominique Michelet. 2016. "The Use of Firewood in Ancient Maya Funerary Rituals: A Case Study from Rio Bec (Campeche, Mexico)." *Latin American Antiquity* 27 (1): 51–73. https://doi.org/10.7183/1045-6635.27.1.51.

Dvořáková, J. Kateřina. 2024. "Experimental Archaeology." In *Encyclopedia of Archaeology* (*Second Edition*), edited by Thilo Rehren and Efthymia Nikita, 284–92. Oxford: Academic Press. https://doi.org/10.1016/B978-0-323-90799-6.00210-X.

Edvardsson, Johannes, Gunnar Almevik, Linda Lindblad, Hans Linderson, and Karl-Magnus Merlin. 2021. "How Cultural Heritage Studies Based on Dendrochronology Can Be Improved through Two-Way Communication." *Forests* 12: 1047. https://doi.org/10.3390/f12081047.

Eschenbrenner Diemer, Gersande, Lisa Sartini, and Margaret Serpico. 2021. "Rediscovering Black Coffins from Deir El-Medina: A Comprehensive Approach إعادة اكتشاف توابيت سوداء من دير المدينة: مقاربة شاملة." *Bulletin de l'Institut Français d'archéologie Orientale* 121 (August): 255–305. https://doi.org/10.4000/bifao.8189.

Fahn, Avraham. 1990. *Plant Anatomy*. 4th ed. New York: Pergamon Press.

Frank, David, Keyan Fang, and Patrick Fonti. 2022. "Dendrochronology: Fundamentals and Innovations." In *Stable Isotopes in Tree Rings: Inferring Physiological, Climatic and Environmental Responses*, edited by Rolf T. W. Siegwolf, J. Renée Brooks, John Roden, and Matthias Saurer, 8: 21–59. Tree Physiology. Cham: Springer International. https://doi.org/10.1007/978-3-030-92698-4.

Fritts, Harold C. 1976. "Chapter 1 – Dendrochronology and Dendroclimatology." In *Tree Rings and Climate*, edited by Harold C. Fritts, 1–54. London: Academic Press. https://doi.org/10.1016/B978-0-12-268450-0.50006-9.

Fritz, Gayle, and Mark Nesbitt. 2014. "Laboratory Analysis and Identification of Plant Macroremains." In *Method and Theory in Paleoethnobotany*, edited by John M. Marston, Jade D'Alpoim Guedes, and Christina Warinner, 115–45. Boulder: University Press of Colorado. https://doi.org/10.5876/9781607323167.c007.

Gale, Rowena, Peter Gasson, Frank Nigel Hepper, and Geoffrey Killen. 2000. "Wood." In *Ancient Egyptian Materials and Technology*, edited by Paul

T. Nicholson and Ian Shaw, 334–71. Cambridge: Cambridge University Press.

Galimberti, Mariagrazia, Christopher Bronk Ramsey, and Sturt W. Manning. 2004. "Wiggle-Match Dating of Tree-Ring Sequences." *Radiocarbon* 46(2): 917–24.

Gallagher, Daphne E. 2014. "Formation Processes of the Macrobotanical Record." In *Method and Theory in Paleoethnobotany*, edited by John M. Marston, Jade D'Alpoim Guedes, and Christina Warinner, 19–34. Boulder: University Press of Colorado.

Goodell, Barry, Jerrold E. Winandy, and Jeffrey J. Morrell. 2020. "Fungal Degradation of Wood: Emerging Data, New Insights and Changing Perceptions." *Coatings* 10(12): 1210. https://doi.org/10.3390/coatings10121210.

Gould, Richard A., and Patty Jo Watson. 1982. "A Dialogue on the Meaning and Use of Analogy in Ethnoarchaeological Reasoning." *Journal of Anthropological Archaeology* 1: 355–81.

Haneca, Kristof, and Koen Deforce. 2020. "Wood Use in Early Medieval Weapon Production." *Archaeological and Anthropological Sciences* 12 (1): 9. https://doi.org/10.1007/s12520-019-01000-5.

Hayes, Kai L., Jason Weinman, Stephen Humphries, David Rubenstein, and Michele L. Koons. 2021. "Evolution of Paleoradiology in Colorado." In *The Egyptian Mummies and Coffins of the Denver Museum of Nature & Science: History, Technical Analysis, and Conservation*, edited by Michele L. Koons and Caroline Arbuckle MacLeod, 52–71. Louisville: University Press of Colorado. https://doi.org/10.5876/9781646421381.c004.

Hedges, John I. 1989. "The Chemistry of Archaeological Wood." In *Archaeological Wood: Properties, Chemistry, and Preservation*, edited by Roger M. Rowell and R. James Barbour, 111–40. Advances in Chemistry 225. American Chemical Society. https://doi.org/10.1021/ba-1990-0225.ch005.

Hoadley, R. Bruce. 1990. *Identifying Wood: Accurate Results with Simple Tools*. A Fine Woodworking Book. Newtown: Taunton Press.

——— 2000. *Understanding Wood: A Craftsman's Guide to Wood Technology*. Revised ed. Newton: The Taunton Press.

Hodder, Ian. 2013. *The Present Past: An Introduction to Anthropology for Archaeologists* (version 2nd Revised ed.). Barnsley: Pen and Sword.

Hoffmann, Per, and Mark A. Jones. 1989. "Structure and Degradation Process for Waterlogged Archaeological Wood." In *Archaeological Wood*, 225: 35–65. Advances in Chemistry 225. American Chemical Society. https://doi.org/10.1021/ba-1990-0225.ch002.

Howley, Kathryn, Caroline Arbuckle MacLeod, and Pearce Paul Creasman. 2021. "Artistic and Textual Analysis of the Third Intermediate Period Coffins at the Denver Museum of Nature & Science." In *The Egyptian Mummies and Coffins of the Denver Museum of Nature & Science: History, Technical Analysis, and Conservation*, edited by Michele L. Koons and Caroline Arbuckle MacLeod, 170–196. Louisville: University Press of Colorado.

IAWA Committee. 1989. "IAWA List of Microscopic Features for Hardwood Identification." *IAWA Journal* 10: 219–332.

——— 2004. "IAWA List of Microscopic Features for Softwood Identification." *IAWA Journal* 25: 1–70.

InsideWood. 2018. "Inside Wood – Search the Inside Wood Database." March 16. http://insidewood.lib.ncsu.edu.

Johns, Dilys A. 2012. *Post-Excavation Treatment Methods for Waterlogged Organic Archaeological Materials*. Oxford: Oxford University Press. https://doi.org/10.1093/oxfordhb/9780199573493.013.0040.

Kaennel, Michèle, and Fritz H. Schweingruber. 1995. *Multilingual Glossary of Dendrochronology: Terms and Definitions in English, German, French, Spanish, Italian, Portuguese and Russian*. Berne Stuttgart Vienna: P. Haupt.

Kaiser, Klaus Felix, Michael Friedrich, Cécile Miramont, et al. 2012. "Challenging Process to Make the Lateglacial Tree-Ring Chronologies from Europe Absolute – an Inventory." *Quaternary Science Reviews*, The INTegration of Ice core, MArine and TErrestrial records of the last termination (INTIMATE) 60,000 to 8000 BP, 36 (March): 78–90. https://doi.org/10.1016/j.quascirev.2010.07.009.

Killen, Geoffrey. 2017. *Ancient Egyptian Furniture Volume I: 4000–1300 BC*. 2nd ed. Vol. 1. Oxford: Oxbow Books.

Koons, Michele L., and Caroline Arbuckle MacLeod, eds. 2021a. *The Egyptian Mummies and Coffins of the Denver Museum of Nature & Science: History, Technical Analysis, and Conservation*. Louisville: University Press of Colorado.

——— 2021b. "Contextualizing the Denver Museum of Nature & Science Mummies and Coffins: A History of Research and Exploring New Narratives." In *The Egyptian Mummies and Coffins of the Denver Museum of Nature & Science: History, Technical Analysis, and Conservation*, edited by Michele K. Koons and Caroline Arbuckle MacLeod, 13–34. Louisville: University Press of Colorado. https://doi.org/10.5876/9781646421381.c002.

Kuniholm, Peter Ian. 2001. "Dendrochronology and Other Applications of Tree-Ring Studies in Archaeology." In *The Handbook of Archaeological Sciences*, edited by Don R. Brothwell and Alan Mark Pollard, 35–46. London: John Wiley & Sons. https://oa.mg/work/2107781206.

Lageard, Jonathan G. A. 2022. "Dendrochronology." In *Encyclopedia of Geoarchaeology*, edited by Allan S. Gilbert, Paul Goldberg, Rolfe D. Mandel, and Vera Aldeias, 1–21. Encyclopedia of Earth Sciences Series. Cham: Springer International. https://doi.org/10.1007/978-3-030-44600-0_41-1.

Lemonnier, Pierre. 1992. *Elements for an Anthropology of Technology*. Anthropological Papers / Museum of Anthropology, University of Michigan, no. 88. Ann Arbor: Museum of Anthropology, University of Michigan.

Mantanis, George I., and Dimitrios Birbilis. 2010. "Physical and Mechanical Properties of Athel Wood (Tamarix Aphylla)." *Turkish Journal of Forestry* 11 (2): 82–87.

Maragoudaki, Eleni. 2019. "'Cutting Edge Technology': New Evidence from Experimentalsimulation and Use of Late Bronze Age Woodworking Cutting Tools. The Saw as 'Case Study.'" In *Experimental Archaeology: Making, Understanding, Story-Telling*, 27–42. Bicester: Archaeopress.

Marston, John M. 2009. "Modeling Wood Acquisition Strategies from Archaeological Charcoal Remains." *Journal of Archaeological Science* 36 (10): 2192–200. https://doi.org/10.1016/j.jas.2009.06.002.

Marston, John M., Jade D'Alpoim Guedes, and Christina Warinner, eds. 2014. *Method and Theory in Paleoethnobotany*. Boulder: University Press of Colorado.

Martín Seijo, María, María Cruz Berrocal, Elena Serrano Herrero, and Chenghwa Tsang. 2021. "Wooden Material Culture and Long-Term Historical Processes in Heping Dao (Keelung, Taiwan)." *Journal of Archaeological Science* 133 (September): 105443. https://doi.org/10.1016/j.jas.2021.105443.

Martinez-Garcia, Jorge, Ingrid Stelzner, Joerg Stelzner, Damian Gwerder, and Philipp Schuetz. 2021. "Automated 3D Tree-Ring Detection and Measurement from X-Ray Computed Tomography." *Dendrochronologia* 69 (October): 125877. https://doi.org/10.1016/j.dendro.2021.125877.

Maxwell, R. Stockton, and Lars-Ake Larsson. 2021. "Measuring Tree-Ring Widths Using the CooRecorder Software Application." *Dendrochronologia* 67 (June): 125841. https://doi.org/10.1016/j.dendro.2021.125841.

Meiggs, Russell. 1982. *Trees and Timber in the Ancient Mediterranean World*. Oxford: Oxford University Press.

Mertz, Mechtild. 2016. *Wood and Traditional Woodworking in Japan*. 2nd ed. Otsu City: Kaiseisha Press.

Mobley, Charles, and Michael Lewis. 2009. "Tree-Ring Analysis of Traditional Native Bark-Stripping at Ship Island, Southeast Alaska, USA." *Vegetation History and Archaeobotany* 18 (May): 261–68. https://doi.org/10.1007/s00334-008-0204-4.

N'Guessan, Jean Louis Lepetit, Bobelé Florence Niamké, N'guessan Jean Claude Yao, and Nadine Amusant. 2023. "Wood Extractives: Main Families, Functional Properties, Fields of Application and Interest of Wood Waste." *Forest Products Journal* 73 (3): 194–208.

Nagy, Nina E., Vincent R. Franceschi, Halvor Solheim, Trygve Krekling, and Erik Christiansen. 2000. "Wound-Induced Traumatic Resin Duct Development in Stems of Norway Spruce (Pinaceae): Anatomy and Cytochemical Traits." *American Journal of Botany* 87 (3): 302–13. https://doi.org/10.2307/2656626.

Newsom, Lee A. 2006. "Paleoenvironmental Aspects of the Macrophytic Plant Assemblage from Page-Ladson." In *First Floridians and Last Mastodons: The Page-Ladson Site in the Aucilla River*, edited by S. David Webb, 181–211. Dordrecht: Springer Netherlands. https://doi.org/10.1007/978-1-4020-4694-0_7.

———. 2022. *Wood in Archaeology*. Cambridge Manuals in Archaeology. Cambridge: Cambridge University Press.

Pearl, Jessie K., John R. Keck, William Tintor, et al. 2020. "New Frontiers in Tree-Ring Research." *The Holocene* 30 (6): 923–41. https://doi.org/10.1177/0959683620902230.

Pearsall, Deborah Marie. 2015. *Paleoethnobotany: A Handbook of Procedures*. 3rd ed. Walnut Creek: Left Coast Press.

Pearson, Charlotte L., Steven W. Leavitt, Bernd Kromer, Sami K Solanki, and Ilya Usoskin. 2022. "Dendrochronology and Radiocarbon Dating." *Radiocarbon* 64 (3): 569–88. https://doi.org/10.1017/RDC.2021.97.

Politis, Gustavo G. 2020. "Ethnoarchaeology." In *Encyclopedia of Global Archaeology*, edited by Claire Smith, 3903–12. Cham: Springer International. https://doi.org/10.1007/978-3-030-30018-0_284.

Pournou, Anastasia. 2020. "Wood Deterioration by Insects." In *Biodeterioration of Wooden Cultural Heritage*, edited by Anastasia Pournou, 425–526. Cham: Springer International. https://doi.org/10.1007/978-3-030-46504-9_7.

Price, Robyn, Vanessa Muros, and Hans Barnard. 2021. "Considerations in the Technical Analysis of Ancient Egyptian Material Remains." In *The Egyptian Mummies and Coffins of the Denver Museum of Nature &*

Science: History, Technical Analysis, and Conservation, edited by Michele K. Koons and Caroline Arbuckle MacLeod, 139–69. Louisville: University Press of Colorado. https://doi.org/10.5876/9781646421381.c008.

Pulak, Cemal. 2001. Cedar for Ships. *Archaeology and History in Lebanon* 14: 24–36.

Raven, Maarten J., Vincent Verschoor, Marije Vugts, and René van Walsem. 2011. *The Memphite Tomb of Horemheb, Commander-in-Chief of Tutankhamun V: The Forecourt and the Area South of the Tomb with Some Notes on the Tomb of Tia*. PALMA 6. Turnhout: Brepols. www.amazon.com/Memphite-Horemheb-Commander-Chief-Tutankhamun/dp/2503531105.

Raven, Peter H., Ray Franklin Evert, and Susan E. Eichhorn. 2013. *Biology of Plants*. 8th ed. New York: W.H. Freeman and Company Publishers.

Reinprecht, Ladislav. 2016. *Wood Deterioration, Protection and Maintenance*. Chichester: Wiley Blackwell.

Rowell, Roger M., and R. James Barbour, eds. 1989. *Archaeology of Wood: Properties, Chemistry, and Preservation*. Advances in Chemistry 225. Washington, D.C.: American Chemical Society. https://doi.org/10.1021/ba-1990-0225.ch005.

Rowell, Roger M., Roger Pettersen, and Mandla A. Tshabalala. 2012. "Cell Wall Chemistry." In *Handbook of Wood Chemistry and Wood Composites*, edited by Roger M. Rowell, 2nd ed., 33–72. London: Routledge Handbooks Online. https://doi.org/10.1201/b12487-5.

Ruffinatto, Flavio, and Alan Crivellaro. 2019. "Identification Key." In *Atlas of Macroscopic Wood Identification: With a Special Focus on Timbers Used in Europe and CITES-Listed Species*, edited by Flavio Ruffinatto, and Alan Crivellaro, 31–35. Cham: Springer International. https://doi.org/10.1007/978-3-030-23566-6_5.

Sands, Rob. 1997. *Prehistoric Woodworking: The Analysis and Interpretation of Bronze and Iron Age Toolmarks*. Wood in Archaeology 1. London: Institute of Archaeology, University College.

Schiffer, Michael B. 1986. "Radiocarbon Dating and the 'Old Wood' Problem: The Case of the Hohokam Chronology." *Journal of Archaeological Science* 13 (1): 13–30. https://doi.org/10.1016/0305-4403(86)90024-5.

Schweingruber, Fritz H. 1988. *Tree Rings*. Dordrecht: Springer Netherlands. https://doi.org/10.1007/978-94-009-1273-1.

———. 1993. *Trees and Wood in Dendrochronology*. Springer Series in Wood Science. Berlin: Springer Berlin Heidelberg. https://doi.org/10.1007/978-3-642-77157-6.

2007. *Wood Structure and Environment*. New York: Springer.

Senalik, Christopher Adam, and Benjamin Farber. 2021. "Commercial Lumber, Round Timbers, and Ties." In *Wood Handbook: Wood as an Engineering Material*, edited by Robert Ross, 6.1–6.25. Madison: U.S. Department of Agriculture. www.fs.usda.gov/research/treesearch/62245.

Shmulsky, Rubin, and Paul David Jones. 2011. *Forest Products and Wood Science: An Introduction*. 6th ed. Chichester: Wiley-Blackwell.

Singh, Adya P., Yoon Soo Kim, and Ramesh R. Chavan. 2019. "Relationship of Wood Cell Wall Ultrastructure to Bacterial Degradation of Wood." Edited by Lloyd A. Donaldson. *IAWA Journal* 40 (4): 845–70. https://doi.org/10.1163/22941932-40190250.

Skibo, James M. 1992. "Ethnoarchaeology, Experimental Archaeology and Inference Building in Ceramic Research." *Archaeologia Polona* 30: 27–38.

Speer, James H. 2010. *Fundamentals of Tree-Ring Research*. Tucson: University of Arizona Press.

Stewart, Hilary. 1995. *Cedar: Tree of Life to the Northwest Coast Indians* (version first paperback pr). First paperback pr. Vancouver: Douglas & McIntyre.

Stuart, Glenn S. L. 2020. "Paleoethnobotany." In *Encyclopedia of Global Archaeology*, edited by Claire Smith, 8312–27. Cham: Springer International. https://doi.org/10.1007/978-3-030-30018-0_2412.

Taylor, R. Ervin 2017. "Radiocarbon Dating." In *Encyclopedia of Geoarchaeology*, edited by Allan S. Gilbert, 689–702. Encyclopedia of Earth Sciences Series. Dordrecht: Springer Netherlands. https://doi.org/10.1007/978-1-4020-4409-0_48.

Tegel, Willy, Bernhard Muigg, Georgios Skiadaresis, Jan Vanmoerkerke, and Andrea Seim. 2022. "Dendroarchaeology in Europe." *Frontiers in Ecology and Evolution* 10 (February): 823622. https://doi.org/10.3389/fevo.2022.823622.

Théry-Parisot, Isabelle, Lucie Chabal, and Julia Chrzavzez. 2010. "Anthracology and Taphonomy, from Wood Gathering to Charcoal Analysis: A Review of the Taphonomic Processes Modifying Charcoal Assemblages, in Archaeological Contexts." *Palaeogeography, Palaeoclimatology, Palaeoecology* 291 (1–2): 142–53. https://doi.org/10.1016/j.palaeo.2009.09.016.

Tullus, Arvo, Malle Mandre, Tea Soo, and Hardi Tullus. 2010. "Relationships between Cellulose, Lignin and Nutrients in the Stemwood of Hybrid Aspen in Estonian Plantations." *Cellulose Chemistry and Technology* 44 (4–6): 101–9.

Ulrich, Roger B. 2007. *Roman Woodworking*. New Haven: Yale University Press.

Van Ham-Meert, Alicia and Aoife Daly. 2023. "Provenancing 16th and 17th Century CE Building Timbers in Denmark – Combining Dendroprovenance and Sr Isotopic Analysis." *pLoS One* 18 (2): 1–22. https://doi.org/10.1371/journal.pone.0278513.

Veal, Robyn. 2017. "The Politics and Economics of Ancient Forests: Timber and Fuel as Levers of Greco-Roman Control." In *Economie Et Inegalite: Ressources, Echanges Et Pouvoir Dans L'Antiquite Classique*, edited by Sitta Von Reden and Pascale Derron, 317–67. Vandoeuvres: Fondation Hardt. Entretiens Sur L'Antiquite Classique De La Fondation Hardt 63. Entretiens sur L'Antiquite' Classique. https://doi.org/10.17863/CAM.13218.

Walsem, René van, Geoffrey T. Martin, Barbara G. Aston, Eugen Strouhal, and Ladislava Horáčková. 1999. "Preliminary Report on the Saqqara Excavations, Season 1999." *Oudheidkunde Medelingen Uit Rijksmuseum van Oudheden Te Leiden* 79: 19–35.

Warner, Richard B. 1990. "A Proposed Adjustment for the 'Old-Wood Effect.'" In *Proceedings of the Second International Symposium 14 C and Archaeology: Groningen 1987*, edited by Willem Gerrit Mook and Harm Tjalling Waterbolk, 159–72. PACT (European Study Group on Physical, Chemical, and Mathematical Techniques Applied to Archaeology); 29. Groningen: Council of Europe. https://books.google.ca/books?id=ifs9xgEACAAJ.

Wendrich, Willeke, ed. 2012. *Archaeology and Apprenticeship: Body Knowledge, Identity, and Communities of Practice*. Tucson: University of Arizona Press.

2013. "Ethnoarchaeology Today: The Relevance of the Discipline from the Egyptian Perspective." In *Contesting Ethnoarchaeologies: Traditions, Theories, Prospects*, edited by Arkadiusz Marciniak and Nurcan Yalman, 191–209. New York: Springer. One World Archaeology 7.

Wheeler, Elisabeth A. 2011. "InsideWood – A Web Resource for Hardwood Anatomy." *IAWA Journal* 32 (2): 199–211.

Wheeler, Elisabeth A., and Pieter Baas. 1998. "Wood Identification – A Review." *IAWA Journal* 19 (3): 241–64.

Wheeler, Elisabeth A., Peter E. Gasson, and Pieter Baas. 2020. "Using the InsideWood Web Site: Potentials and Pitfalls." *IAWA Journal* 41 (4): 412–62.

White, Chantel E., and China P. Shelton. 2014. "Recovering Macrobotanical Remains: Current Methods and Techniques." In *Method and Theory in Paleoethnobotany*, edited by John M. Marston, Jade D'Alpoim Guedes, and Christina Warinner, 95–114. Boulder: University Press of Colorado. https://doi.org/10.5876/9781607323167.c006.

Wiedenhoeft, Alex C. 2012. "Structure and Function of Wood." In *Handbook of Wood Chemistry and Wood Composites*, edited by Roger M. Rowell, 2nd ed., 9–32. Boca Raton: CRC Press. https://doi.org/10.1201/b12487.

Williams, Donald C. 2008. "'Reading' Tool Marks on Furniture." *The Chronicle of the Early American Industries Association* 61 (3): 106–16.

Wright, Patti J. 2005. "Flotation Samples and Some Paleoethnobotanical Implications." *Journal of Archaeological Science* 32 (1): 19–26. https://doi.org/10.1016/j.jas.2004.06.003.

WOOD Magazine Staff. 2021. "When Wood goes Bad: How to Deal with Warped Boards." *Wood* (March 16, 2021). https://www.woodmagazine.com/wood-supplies/lumber/when-good-wood-goes-bad.

Wylie, Alison. 1985. "The Reaction against Analogy." *Advances in Archaeological Method and Theory* 8: 63–111.

Acknowledgements

I would like to express my gratitude to the Denver Museum of Nature & Science, the Museo Egizio in Turin, the National Museum of Antiquities (RMO) in Leiden, and the Egyptian Ministry of Tourism and Antiquities for supporting my research efforts and providing access to the wooden objects discussed within this work. My thanks also to Duncan MacLeod, Glenn Stuart, Hannah Herrick, section editor Hans Barnard, and the anonymous reviewers for making helpful suggestions for improvements to earlier drafts of this work.

Cambridge Elements

Current Archaeological Tools and Techniques

Hans Barnard
Cotsen Institute of Archaeology

Hans Barnard was associate adjunct professor in the Department of Near Eastern Languages and Cultures as well as associate researcher at the Cotsen Institute of Archaeology, both at the University of California, Los Angeles. He currently works at the Roman site of Industria in northern Italy and previously participated in archaeological projects in Armenia, Chile, Egypt, Ethiopia, Italy, Iceland, Panama, Peru, Sudan, Syria, Tunisia, and Yemen. This is reflected in the seven books and more than 100 articles and chapters to which he contributed.

Willeke Wendrich
Polytechnic University of Turin

Willeke Wendrich is Professor of Cultural Heritage and Digital Humanities at the Politecnico di Torino (Turin, Italy). Until 2023 she was Professor of Egyptian Archaeology and Digital Humanities at the University of California, Los Angeles, and the first holder of the Joan Silsbee Chair in African Cultural Archaeology. Between 2015 and 2023 she was Director of the Cotsen Institute of Archaeology, with which she remains affiliated. She managed archaeological projects in Egypt, Ethiopia, Italy, and Yemen, and is on the board of the International Association of Egyptologists, Museo Egizio (Turin, Italy), the Institute for Field Research, and the online UCLA Encyclopedia of Egyptology.

About the Series

Cambridge University Press and the Cotsen Institute of Archaeology at UCLA collaborate on this series of Elements, which aims to facilitate deployment of specific techniques by archaeologists in the field and in the laboratory. It provides readers with a basic understanding of selected techniques, followed by clear instructions how to implement them, or how to collect samples to be analyzed by a third party, and how to approach interpretation of the results.

Cambridge Elements⎯

Current Archaeological Tools and Techniques

Elements in the Series

Archaeological Mapping and Planning
Hans Barnard

Mobile Landscapes and Their Enduring Places
Bruno David, Jean-Jacques Delannoy and Jessie Birkett-Rees

Cultural Burning
Bruno David, Michael-Shawn Fletcher, Simon Connor, Virginia Ruth Pullin, Jessie Birkett-Rees, Jean-Jacques Delannoy, Michela Mariani, Anthony Romano and S. Yoshi Maezumi

Knowledge Discovery from Archaeological Materials
Pedro A. López-García, Denisse L. Argote, Manuel A. Torres-García and Michael C. Thrun

Machine Learning for Archaeological Applications in R
Denisse L. Argote, Pedro A. López-García, Manuel A. Torres-García and Michael C. Thrun

Worked Bone, Antler, Ivory, and Keratinous Materials
Adam DiBattista

Infrared Spectroscopy of Archaeological Sediments
Michael B. Toffolo

Retrospective and Prospective for Scientific Provenance Studies in Archaeology
A.M. Pollard

Archaeological Wood and Woodworking
Caroline Arbuckle MacLeod

A full series listing is available at: www.cambridge.org/EATT

For EU product safety concerns, contact us at Calle de José Abascal, 56–1°, 28003 Madrid, Spain or eugpsr@cambridge.org.

www.ingramcontent.com/pod-product-compliance
Ingram Content Group UK Ltd.
Pitfield, Milton Keynes, MK11 3LW, UK
UKHW031017290425
457986UK00019B/726